Devotions to Go

ZONDERVAN®
.com

ZONDERVAN

Devotions to Go, Volume Two
Copyright © 2009 by Zondervan

Requests for information should be addressed to:
Zondervan, *Grand Rapids, Michigan 49530*

ISBN 978-0-310-82281-3

Interior design by Steve Culver

Printed in China

_____

09 10 11 12 13 14 15 • 23 22 21 20 19 18 17 16 15 14 13 12 11 10 9 8 7 6 5 4 3 2 1

Mark 2:23-28

One Sabbath Jesus was going through the grainfields, and as his disciples walked along, they began to pick some heads of grain. The Pharisees said to him, "Look, why are they doing what is unlawful on the Sabbath?"

He answered, "Have you never read what David did when he and his companions were hungry and in need? In the days of Abiathar the high priest, he entered the house of God and ate the con-secrated bread, which is lawful only for priests to eat. And he also gave some to his companions."

Then he said to them, "The Sabbath was made for man, not man for the Sabbath. So the Son of Man is Lord even of the Sabbath."

Jesus often upset the religious establishment of his day. He challenged the Pharisees' rules about what could and could not be done on the Sabbath. And there were lots of rules and lots of Jewish leaders watching and enforcing those rules.

Did you have rules growing up about what you could and couldn't do on Sunday, the day that Christians have traditionally viewed as the parallel of the Old Testament Jewish Saturday Sabbath (see Acts 20:7; 1 Corinthians 16:2)? Whatever your past, in marriage you have to merge two potentially conflicting sets of expectations. Instead of arguing over whose history is more meaningful, why not wipe both slates clean and create a fresh approach based on Jesus' statement that the Sabbath was made for us?

A good place to start might be with the premise that the Sabbath is a gift from God, not an obligation. So we don't *have* to do anything. With that thought in mind, we might think of the Sabbath as dinner at a fine restaurant. On this special day we get to sort through a full menu of delights to feed our spirits, minds and bodies. For example, besides worship, church also offers fellowship and service.

Deuteronomy 15:7-8

If there is a poor man among your brothers in any of the towns of the land that the L<small>ORD</small> your God is giving you, do not be hardhearted or tightfisted toward your poor brother. Rather be openhanded and freely lend him whatever he needs.

Openhearted and openhanded

There is much suffering in the world—very much. Material suffering, suffering from hunger, suffering from homelessness, suffering from all kinds of diseases. But the greatest suffering is being lonely, just having no one and feeling unloved. In these times the whole world runs and is hurried, and there are some who fall down on the way and have no strength to go ahead. These are the ones we must care about.

Let us be very sincere in our dealings with each other and have the courage to accept each other as we are. Do not be surprised at or become preoccupied with each other's failures. Rather, see and find the good in each other, for each one of us is created in the image of God.

Be kind in your actions. Do not think that you are the only one who can do efficient work. This makes you harsh in your judgment of others who may not have the same talents. Do your best and trust that others do their best. And be faithful in small things because it is in them that your strength lies. In loving one another through our works we bring an increase of grace and a growth in divine love.

While Jesus was in one of the towns, a man came along who was covered with leprosy. When he saw Jesus, he fell with his face to the ground and begged him, "Lord, if you are willing, you can make me clean."

Jesus reached out his hand and touched the man. "I am willing," he said. "Be clean!" And immediately the leprosy left him.

Then Jesus ordered him, "Don't tell anyone, but go, show yourself to the priest and offer the sacrifices that Moses commanded for your cleansing, as a testimony to them."

Yet the news about him spread all the more, so that crowds of people came to hear him and to be healed of their sicknesses. But Jesus often withdrew to lonely places and prayed.

The story of Jesus and the man with leprosy in Luke 5 is a powerful example of Jesus' ability to heal and change lives. But we also learn something else about Jesus in this story— he got tired. Not tired of helping people, just tired, period.

In his weariness, Jesus would pull away from the crowd and even from his friends to find a quiet place where he could rest his body and renew his spirit. Surely, this was a necessity, not a luxury. Jesus understood that making time to be alone with God wasn't selfish. And he didn't do it just so he could be a more effective minister to others. Jesus stepped away from the crowd because he needed to. This was Jesus at his most human—tired and in need of restoration.

We seem to have this idea that marriage, particularly a new marriage, should be all about togetherness. But when a couple spends all their free time together, something else suffers. Maybe old friends get pushed aside. Maybe quiet moments for personal reflection or prayer get overlooked. Being together has obvious rewards. But being alone from time to time can be the key to keeping us in balance.

Genesis 19:26

*But Lot's wife looked back, and
she became a pillar of salt.*

L ot's wife wasn't able to let go of her home in Sodom, even though God sent angels to warn her family to run for their lives because judgment was coming.

It's difficult to leave the familiar behind. That fact is as true today as it was in the days of Sodom and Gomorrah's destruction—even when God himself is saying, "It's time to move on." If you've ever struggled with a destructive habit, you've felt the pull of the familiar just as you've sensed God's nudge to "Stop. Let Go."

Unlike Lot's wife, none of us has ever become a pillar of salt by turning back for one last peek. Yet we all struggle with the difficulties of letting go of the old in order to grasp the new. Take heart, God understands that letting go of the familiar is hard. But he has called us to move on to a new life in Jesus Christ by letting go of our old worldly lives, our old habits and our old dreams, to boldly move forward without looking back. When you feel God's call to move, allow him to guide you. He will give you the grace to do whatever he has asked.

The next morning the Jews formed a conspiracy and bound themselves with an oath not to eat or drink until they had killed Paul. More than forty men were involved in this plot. They went to the chief priests and elders and said, "We have taken a solemn oath not to eat anything until we have killed Paul. Now then, you and the Sanhedrin petition the commander to bring him before you on the pretext of wanting more accurate information about his case. We are ready to kill him before he gets here."

But when the son of Paul's sister heard of this plot, he went into the barracks and told Paul.

Then Paul called one of the centurions and said, "Take this young man to the commander; he has something to tell him."

The commander took the young man by the hand, drew him aside and asked, "What is it you want to tell me?"

He said: "The Jews have agreed to ask you to bring Paul before the Sanhedrin tomorrow on the pretext of wanting more accurate information about him. Don't give in to them, because more than forty of them are waiting in ambush for him."

Paul's preaching had gotten him into a lot of trouble. A mob of men had banded together and formed a plan to murder him. When Paul's nephew heard about the plot he risked his life to warn Paul and report the matter to the commanding officer. Paul's nephew wasn't just whistle-blowing, he was busting up a conspiracy ring straight out of a spy movie. This was one young man versus forty thugs who were so vehement in their hatred of Paul that they had made a pact to fast until he was dead! Even the commanding officer sensed the danger and urged Paul's nephew to keep his actions secret.

It's possible that at some point in your married life you'll be faced with a situation like this—one that involves danger, risk or sacrifice, and you'll have an opportunity to make a heroic choice to help your spouse. But in everyday life, often the tougher challenge comes by way of the thankless, humdrum, non-dramatic opportunities you have to help your spouse and stick by him or her. It isn't always thrilling to help, but that's just what married people do.

Job 9:2-6, 12-14, 32-35

*How can a mortal be righteous
  before God?*
*Though one wished to dispute
  with him,*
*he could not answer him one time
  out of a thousand.*
*His wisdom is profound, his power
  is vast.*
*Who has resisted him and come
  out unscathed?*
*He moves mountains without their
  knowing it and overturns them
  in his anger.*
*He shakes the earth from its place
  and makes its pillars tremble.*

*If he snatches away, who can
  stop him?*
*Who can say to him, "What are
  you doing?"*
God does not restrain his anger;
*even the cohorts of Rahab cowered
  at his feet.*
How then can I dispute with him?
*How can I find words
  to argue with him?*

*He is not a man like me that I might
  answer him,*
*that we might confront each other
  in court.*
*If only there were someone to
  arbitrate between us,*
to lay his hand upon us both,
*someone to remove God's rod
  from me,*
*so that his terror would frighten me
  no more.*
*Then I would speak up without fear
  of him,*
*but as it now stands with me,
  I cannot.*

he death of Job's children and the loss of all he possessed were unexplainable from a human perspective. It just didn't seem fair. Job longed to argue with God and plead his case, but he realized that God "is not a man like me that I might answer him." So, he longed for someone to arbitrate between them.

As mere mortals it's simply not possible to look beyond heaven's veil to see why God allows things to happen as they do. The simple truth is that God is God and we are not. And let's face it, sometimes the things that happen truly don't seem fair. But thankfully, God has sent an arbitrator in the form of his Son, Jesus Christ, to mediate between humans and our holy God. The Bible tells us that Jesus "is able to save completely those who come to God through him, because he always lives to intercede for them" (Hebrews 7:25).

Though we may suffer temporarily on this earth—and no one is denying the intense grief we experience as human beings—through faith in Christ we can rest assured of an eternity where "there will be no more death or mourning or crying or pain" (Revelation 21:4).

Mark 5:25-34

And a woman was there who had been subject to bleeding for twelve years. She had suffered a great deal under the care of many doctors and had spent all she had, yet instead of getting better she grew worse. When she heard about Jesus, she came up behind him in the crowd and touched his cloak, because she thought, "If I just touch his clothes, I will be healed." Immediately her bleeding stopped and she felt in her body that she was freed from her suffering.

At once Jesus realized that power had gone out from him. He turned around in the crowd and asked, "Who touched my clothes?"

"You see the people crowding against you," his disciples answered, "and yet you can ask, 'Who touched me?'"

But Jesus kept looking around to see who had done it. Then the woman, knowing what had happened to her, came and fell at his feet and, trembling with fear, told him the whole truth. He said to her, "Daughter, your faith has healed you. Go in peace and be freed from your suffering."

"If I only touch his cloak …" How great was her faith in the Master! She surmised she only had to graze his power in order to be changed. She willingly believed that he would not require her to go to great lengths to receive what she needed. She did not intend to jump through hoops, recite a mantra or go through the motions to receive mercy. Her approach was simple and heartfelt. If reaching out to him in faith did not work, she had no other option.

"If I only touch his cloak …" She knew the source of the power. Those whom she'd sought assistance from before—doctors, priests, family and friends—had only let her down. None could give her relief. But when she saw Jesus and witnessed his miracles firsthand, she knew he was the One who would not disappoint. The disciples and the host of followers surrounding him may have intimidated her, but they did not distract her. She did not pull one of them aside and issue her request. She was laser-focused on the Father's Son.

"If I only touch his cloak, I will be healed." She did, and she was.

Micah 6:6-8

With what shall I come before the
Lord and bow down before the exalted God?
Shall I come before him with burnt offerings,
with calves a year old?

Will the Lord be pleased with thousands of rams,
with ten thousand rivers of oil?
Shall I offer my firstborn for my transgression,
the fruit of my body for the sin of my soul?

He has showed you, O man, what is good.
And what does the Lord require of you?
To act justly and to love mercy
and to walk humbly with your God.

Picture a courtroom. The judge enters the room, his long robe flowing. At first you can't see his face. But when he sits down at the bench his identity is revealed. God is the judge, and his people are on trial.

What can they do to find favor with God? Is there a sacrifice they can make? What penance is required? The people have tried to pacify him with large and costly offerings. But Micah reminds us that God sees the heart. He knows these are not genuine and humble expressions of repentance. He sees that the sacrifices are an attempt to replace approaching God honestly.

Giving tithes, attending church regularly and teaching are all good things, but they cannot take the place of identifying so closely with God that we almost automatically do that which is closest to his heart: Act justly, love mercy and walk humbly with God. That's what obedience really is. And obedience, which can sound like a dutiful word, or a guiding business exchange, should be a joyful word. It becomes so when we stop calculating the cost of doing what God commands and instead respond with abandon to the One who loves us.

2 Kings 22:15-20

The prophet Huldah said to them, "This is what the L ord, the God of Israel, says: Tell the man who sent you to me, 'This is what the L ord says: I am going to bring disaster on this place and its people, according to everything written in the book the king of Judah has read. Because they have forsaken me and burned incense to other gods and provoked me to anger by all the idols their hands have made, my anger will burn against this place and will not be quenched.' Tell the king of Judah, who sent you to inquire of the L ord, 'This is what the L ord, the God of Israel, says concerning the words you heard:

Because your heart was responsive and you humbled yourself before the L ord when you heard what I have spoken against this place and its people, that they would become accursed and laid waste, and because you tore your robes and wept in my presence, I have heard you, declares the L ord. Therefore I will gather you to your fathers, and you will be buried in peace. Your eyes will not see all the disaster I am going to bring on this place.' "

Ready in a pinch. That was Huldah, a prophetess in Judah. The thing about being one of God's messengers was that the people usually didn't turn to her until it was a time of crisis. When the people needed to hear a word from God, they turned to the resident prophetess for answers. This last minute urgency didn't rattle her. It came with the territory.

Never knowing when she would need to share a word of wisdom or petition the Lord on the people's behalf, she had to stay prepared. She couldn't slack off, spiritually speaking. She drew strength by reminding herself that she couldn't afford to miss an opportunity to be available and useful to God. And on this day, she was able to deliver the timely and sensitive message that God wanted Judah to hear.

Like Huldah, we never know when someone will show up on our doorstep seeking spiritual wisdom. Sometimes it's your friend or neighbor, but it can be a stranger, too. No matter who shows up, God has a word for them. And it's good to be prepared.

While Jesus was in Bethany in the home of a man known as Simon the Leper, a woman came to him with an alabaster jar of very expensive perfume, which she poured on his head as he was reclining at the table.

When the disciples saw this, they were indignant. "Why this waste?" they asked. "This perfume could have been sold at a high price and the money given to the poor."

Aware of this, Jesus said to them, "Why are you bothering this woman? She has done a beautiful thing to me. The poor you will always have with you, but you will not always have me. When she poured this perfume on my body, she did it to prepare me for burial. I tell you the truth, wherever this gospel is preached throughout the world, what she has done will also be told, in memory of her."

Extravagant love

his scene in Matthew continues to be an example of extravagant love. We know from John's Gospel that the woman mentioned here is Mary of Bethany, the sister of Lazarus and Martha. This event took place during the final week of Jesus' life after he had raised Mary's brother from the dead and wept with her and her sister.

Why did Mary pour out the perfume? Perhaps she had followed Christ and heard his predictions about the signs of end times. Maybe she had heard him tell the parable of the ten virgins. She might have sensed that something was different about Jesus that night. Although she may not have understood the full meaning of Jesus' words, Mary poured out her expensive perfume from an alabaster jar, anointing Jesus with her love. Most likely, she gave her Lord the most valuable thing she possessed. Though others criticized her, Jesus praised her for her extravagant expression of love for him, for preparing him for his burial in a symbolic way.

What is your most precious possession? Are you willing to pour out your time? Your money? Your gifts? Your talents? When you give your best to Jesus, he will accept your offering of extravagant love with joy.

Jeremiah 31:31-34

"The time is coming," declares the LORD, "when I will make a new covenant with the house of Israel and with the house of Judah.

It will not be like the covenant I made with their forefathers when I took them by the hand to lead them out of Egypt, because they broke my covenant, though I was a husband to them," declares the LORD.

"This is the covenant I will make with the house of Israel after that time," declares the LORD. "I will put my law in their minds and write it on their hearts. I will be their God, and they will be my people.

"No longer will a man teach his neighbor, or a man his brother, saying, 'Know the LORD,' because they will all know me, from the least of them to the greatest," declares the LORD. "For I will forgive their wickedness and will remember their sins no more."

O ur days are filled with juggling and struggling. We struggle to get the kids to school on time, to get to the office on time and then to get back home on time. We contend with our schedules to get the house clean, the projects done, the meals made and the mortgage paid. In the midst of the tumult and pressure, it's hard to fit it all in.

The reality is, we don't always "want" God enough to fit him into our schedule. We will never get closer to God if we rely on our effort and willpower alone. Jeremiah reminds us of a life-changing truth: God wants to be near us. In the midst of your working, pushing and hurrying, the God of the universe isn't waiting for an opening in your schedule. He has already come to you.

What does it look like to respond to his desire for intimacy? It might mean simply acknowledging his presence, recognizing the truth already written on your heart. It might mean enjoying the freedom that comes when you quit striving and working and rest in the power of his presence and forgiveness. No matter how you respond, know that he is there waiting for you.

Isaiah 35:4, 8-10

Say to those with fearful hearts,
    "Be strong, do not fear;
    your God will come,
    he will come with vengeance;
    with divine retribution
    he will come to save you."

And a highway will be there;
    it will be called the Way
    of Holiness.
    The unclean will not journey on it;
    it will be for those who walk in
    that Way;
    wicked fools will not go about
    on it.

No lion will be there,
    nor will any ferocious beast get
    up on it;

they will not be found there.
    But only the redeemed
    will walk there,

and the ransomed of the LORD
    will return.
They will enter Zion with singing;
everlasting joy will crown
    their heads.
Gladness and joy will
    overtake them,
and sorrow and sighing will
    flee away.

Anyone who has ever taken a road trip with small children can anticipate the question. Kids seldom understand the concept of time and distance. It might be many miles yet to Grandma's house, but restless children pepper their parents with questions before they've even reached the expressway. "Are we there yet?"

Scripture often describes our lives in terms of a spiritual journey. Some stretches of our spiritual roadway are straight and smooth; others are marred by a habitual sin, a time of distance from God or another difficulty that makes our path rocky. Isaiah wrote of a different kind of highway, a highway of holiness. In biblical times, certain roads between temples could only be used by those who were ceremonially clean. Therefore, "the Way of Holiness" refers to an actual, literal road.

Spiritually speaking, we are on a path that is leading somewhere. When it comes to our final destination, none of us is "there yet," but we have God's Word to lead us in the right direction. Author and speaker Patsy Clairmont wrote, "I don't know where the long and winding road is leading you, but I do know this: if you remember passing Calvary, you are on the right road."

Job 40:1, 8-14

The Lord said to Job:

"Would you discredit my justice?
Would you condemn
me to justify yourself?

"Do you have an arm like God's,
and can your voice thunder
like his?

"Then adorn yourself with glory
and splendor,
and clothe yourself in
honor and majesty.

"Unleash the fury of your wrath,
look at every proud
man and bring him low,

look at every proud man and
humble him,
crush the wicked where
they stand.

"Bury them all in the dust together;
shroud their faces in the grave.

Then I myself will admit to you
that your own right hand can
save you."

W ho hasn't wanted to shake her fist at God and scream, "Why?"

When we consider the mystery of suffering, the story of Job inevitably comes to mind. At this point in the story, Job has suffered horribly, and he has boldly questioned God, protesting that he didn't deserve to lose his family, his health and his possessions. Well-intentioned friends have come alongside him, offering unhelpful explanations and pat answers. Job has cried out to God, and God has answered him with amazing words. The Lord challenged him with questions that reveal Job's limitations. Job began to understand and bowed his head in silence to the Creator of the universe.

But notice something. God loved Job enough to be with him in his suffering—and that made all the difference. Job didn't need to keep asking the questions because he had discovered that God himself was the answer. He didn't need the specifics; he finally rested in the truth that God is God, and that was enough.

Sometimes, when we reach the end of ourselves, when we reach the end of the tears and the rage and the questions, when we are quiet, we hear him say, "I am God. I am here."

Ephesians 1:11-17

In him we were also chosen, having been predestined according to the plan of him who works out everything in conformity with the purpose of his will, in order that we, who were the first to hope in Christ, might be for the praise of his glory. And you also were included in Christ when you heard the word of truth, the gospel of your salvation. Having believed, you were marked in him with a seal, the promised Holy Spirit, who is a deposit guaranteeing our inheritance until the redemption of those who are God's possession—to the praise of his glory.

For this reason, ever since I heard about your faith in the Lord Jesus and your love for all the saints, I have not stopped giving thanks for you, remembering you in my prayers. I keep asking that the God of our Lord Jesus Christ, the glorious Father, may give you the Spirit of wisdom and revelation, so that you may know him better.

Be thankful for each other

Paul began his letter to the Ephesians by addressing them as the faithful in Christ Jesus. Next, he told them that they had been chosen and adopted by God to be holy and blameless, and it was God's pleasure to have chosen them. Paul said that God's grace had been lavished on them, they had been marked with the seal of the Holy Spirit, and they were God's possession. "For this reason," Paul said, "ever since I heard about your faith in the Lord Jesus and your love for all his people, I have not stopped giving thanks for you, remembering you in my prayers."

Imagine getting such a beautiful message from your spouse. How would you feel as your spouse expressed the things he or she appreciates about you? Imagine someone saying, "I'm continually giving thanks for you. Every time I think of you I thank God for who you are and what you mean to me. My life is better because of you, and I remember you daily in my prayers."

If your spouse said that to you, you might hold your head a little higher, walk with a little more bounce in your step, smile more. Being grateful for your spouse will make him or her grateful in return.

"When I came to the spring today, I said, 'O LORD, God of my master Abraham, if you will, please grant success to the journey on which I have come. See, I am standing beside this spring; if a maiden comes out to draw water and I say to her, "Please let me drink a little water from your jar," and if she says to me, "Drink, and I'll draw water for your camels too," let her be the one the LORD has chosen for my master's son.'

"Before I finished praying in my heart, Rebekah came out, with her jar on her shoulder. She went down to the spring and drew water, and I said to her, 'Please give me a drink.'

"She quickly lowered her jar from her shoulder and said, 'Drink, and I'll water your camels too.' So I drank, and she watered the camels also.

Laban and Bethuel answered, "This is from the LORD. Here is Rebekah; take her and go, and let her become the wife of your master's son, as the LORD has directed."

So they called Rebekah and asked her, "Will you go with this man?"

"I will go," she said.

The story of Isaac and Rebekah is all about people making choices. Think about it: Wouldn't it have been easier for Abraham to choose a wife for his son from among local families he already knew? Yes, but Abraham chose to obey God's directive that his family not intermarry with the Canaanites. His servant chose to accept a complicated challenge from his employer, trusting God to lead him to the right woman.

And Rebekah had to make a decision that would affect the rest of her life. She ultimately chose to trust her life and future to the servant of a distant relative whose God was her God. The story of the divinely arranged marriage between Isaac and Rebekah reminds us that nothing is too difficult for God.

Trust and obey—these two words go together like coffee and cream. Yet every day we face difficult situations that seem to defy simple solutions. How do we determine the right choice? Obey the guidance you find in God's Word, earnestly pray and seek trusted counsel, then trust God with the outcome. Will you have it your way or God's way? First trust God to have your best interest at heart, and then trust him to lead you to the right choice.

She said to him, "How can you say, 'I love you,' when you won't confide in me? This is the third time you have made a fool of me and haven't told me the secret of your great strength." With such nagging she prodded him day after day until he was tired to death.

So he told her everything. "No razor has ever been used on my head," he said, "because I have been a Nazirite set apart to God since birth. If my head were shaved, my strength would leave me, and I would become as weak as any other man."

When Delilah saw that he had told her everything, she sent word to the rulers of the Philistines, "Come back once more; he has told me everything." So the rulers of the Philistines returned with the silver in their hands. Having put him to sleep on her lap, she called a man to shave off the seven braids of his hair, and so began to subdue him. And his strength left him.

The Philistines seized him, gouged out his eyes and took him to Gaza. Binding him with bronze shackles, they set him to grinding in the prison.

Femme fatales

A femme fatale is a woman who uses her powers of seduction to lure a man into a dangerous or compromising situation. In the Bible we meet Delilah who used her influence to discover the secrets of one of Israel's judges, Samson.

Delilah's story shows how men can be swayed by women's wiles and their own desires. Delilah used her sexual attraction and her cunning to bring a man down—for a price. She relentlessly manipulated Samson in order to get the information she needed. When he finally revealed the truth, she rushed to the Philistine rulers to gather her reward. In a heartbeat Samson lost not just his strength, but the divine gift God had bestowed upon him.

We think it would be great to be able to get our husbands, boyfriends, coworkers, etc. to do what we want. And perhaps, sometimes, we do use feminine wiles, manipulation and nagging to get our way. But are such methods honest? Are they loving? Wouldn't it be better to be the kind of woman others can trust? How much better to employ honesty, kindness and patience to build up the men we love, rather than trample them in the pursuit of our selfish desires.

Elijah went before the people and said, "How long will you waver between two opinions? If the Lord is God, follow him; but if Baal is God, follow him."

Then Elijah said to them, "I am the only one of the Lord's prophets left, but Baal has four hundred and fifty prophets. Get two bulls for us. Let them choose one for themselves, and let them cut it into pieces and put it on the wood but not set fire to it. I will prepare the other bull and put it on the wood but not set fire to it. Then you call on the name of your god, and I will call on the name of the Lord. The god who answers by fire—he is God."

At the time of sacrifice, Elijah stepped forward and prayed: "O Lord, God of Abraham, Isaac and Israel, let it be known today that you are God in Israel and that I am your servant and have done all these things at your command. Answer me, O Lord, answer me, so these people will know that you, O Lord, are God, and that you are turning their hearts back again."

Balancing act?

The prophet Elijah confronted the people of his day and demanded they choose whom they would serve—the true God of Israel or the false gods of the pagan nations surrounding them. Basically, he challenged them, "Get off the fence! You can't have it both ways."

Most of us have never been put in a position in which we had to choose between worshipping the true God or bowing down to statues made of wood or stone. Yet we often find ourselves tempted to try that balancing act while living in a spiritually and morally bankrupt culture. We neglect to say the things we know we should and then excuse ourselves by saying we will let our faith be seen in our actions rather than heard in our words. At times these may be legitimate claims, but at other times they may be nothing more than convenient excuses so we don't have to risk rejection.

Elijah wasn't concerned with rejection when he challenged the false prophets and called the people to serve the true God. He put it all on the line—even his life. The prophet refused to compromise or put himself in the precarious position of riding the fence. As a result, God vindicated him in the sight of his enemies.

2 Timothy 2:15-19, 22-24

Do your best to present yourself to God as one approved, a workman who does not need to be ashamed and who correctly handles the word of truth. Avoid godless chatter, because those who indulge in it will become more and more ungodly. Their teaching will spread like gangrene. Among them are Hymenaeus and Philetus, who have wandered away from the truth. They say that the resurrection has already taken place, and they destroy the faith of some. Nevertheless, God's solid foundation stands firm, sealed with this inscription: "The Lord knows those who are his," and, "Everyone who confesses the name of the Lord must turn away from wickedness."

Flee the evil desires of youth, and pursue righteousness, faith, love and peace, along with those who call on the Lord out of a pure heart. Don't have anything to do with foolish and stupid arguments, because you know they produce quarrels. And the Lord's servant must not quarrel; instead, he must be kind to everyone, able to teach, not resentful.

When we gossip we're a lot like slimy salamanders slinking around corners and shedding bits of rotting tissue. "Godless chatter" is important to think about in all our relationships, but it holds special significance for marriages. The more we interact with each other, the more potential we have for either encouraging or discouraging each other. We can affirm each other's choices or erode each other's spirits with silly suspicions, nagging or doubts.

A word spoken against another is not usually the starting point of gossip. It is only when someone picks up the negative baton and starts running with it that gossip begins.

Godless chatter is an option, not a necessity. Paul said we have a choice in the matter. And the choice begins at home. We can indulge in gossip and become more ungodly, or we can end it and extend grace instead of a critical spirit toward others, thereby growing in godliness with our gracious Savior, Jesus Christ, and with each other.

Now Laban had two daughters; the name of the older was Leah, and the name of the younger was Rachel. Leah had weak eyes, but Rachel was lovely in form, and beautiful. Jacob was in love with Rachel and said, "I'll work for you seven years in return for your younger daughter Rachel."

Laban said, "It's better that I give her to you than to some other man. Stay here with me." So Jacob served seven years to get Rachel, but they seemed like only a few days to him because of his love for her.

Then Jacob said to Laban, "Give me my wife. My time is completed, and I want to lie with her."

So Laban brought together all the people of the place and gave a feast. But when evening came, he took his daughter Leah and gave her to Jacob, and Jacob lay with her.

When morning came, there was Leah! So Jacob said to Laban, "What is this you have done to me? I served you for Rachel, didn't I? Why have you deceived me?"

*L*eah came to her wedding night cloaked under layers of bridal veils. But her cover didn't last long. Morning came and her true identity came to light. Jacob was shocked to find that he had been deceived into marrying his beloved Rachel's sister.

The Bible places the blame squarely on Laban's shoulders. But did Leah play any part in the deceit? Was she simply obeying a conniving father in a last-ditch effort to win a lover, or was she seeking to spite a sister more beautiful than she? We will never know what kept Leah quiet as she went to marry Jacob, disguised beneath veils and robes, bangles and jewels. But we do know that in the clear light of morning the game was up for the whole family.

Do you feel that you have to hide your true self to gain a relationship? It could be that, like Leah, you fear that you are unlovely compared to others. But God created you, and that's why you are both lovely and lovable just as you are. So ask God for the courage to remove the veils covering your heart and recognize the beauty of his image in you.

When the Lord was about to take Elijah up to heaven in a whirlwind, Elijah and Elisha were on their way from Gilgal. Elijah said to Elisha, "Stay here; the Lord has sent me to Bethel." But Elisha said, "As surely as the Lord lives and as you live, I will not leave you." So they went down to Bethel.

As they were walking along and talking together, suddenly a chariot of fire and horses of fire appeared and separated the two of them, and Elijah went up to heaven in a whirlwind. Elisha saw this and cried out, "My father! My father! The chariots and horsemen of Israel!" And Elisha saw him no more. Then he took hold of his own clothes and tore them apart.

He picked up the cloak that had fallen from Elijah and went back and stood on the bank of the Jordan. Then he took the cloak that had fallen from him and struck the water with it. "Where now is the Lord, the God of Elijah?" he asked. When he struck the water, it divided to the right and to the left, and he crossed over.

E lisha had steadfastly stayed with his mentor Elijah. Even when Elijah commanded Elisha to remain in Bethel, Elisha refused, saying he would never leave the older prophet's side. Thus, Elisha expressed his love and faithfulness not only to Elijah but also to God. Elisha vowed never to leave Elijah, and he didn't until he had gleaned everything he needed to know from this godly man, until he received the blessing of his mentor, until he watched his mentor vanish in a heavenly whirlwind.

We all need mentors like Elijah: men and women who have faced challenges and overcome; men and women who have grown through struggle and perseverance; men and women who have seen God perform miracles; men and women who have gone through hard times and experienced God's presence with them. These are the men and women who can pass on the news that God's Word is still active and dynamic among us.

Who are the godly men and women walking along the roads in your life who are willing to pass on the knowledge they've gained? Who has watched you as you've worked in your Bible study, your volunteer work or at your job? Who has seen your gifts and your potential? Try doing what Elisha did—follow him or her and glean their knowledge of the living God concerning how to best serve him.

Jesus went up on a mountainside and called to him those he wanted, and they came to him. He appointed twelve—designating them apostles—that they might be with him and that he might send them out to preach and to have authority to drive out demons. These are the twelve he appointed: Simon (to whom he gave the name Peter); James son of Zebedee and his brother John (to them he gave the name Boanerges, which means Sons of Thunder); Andrew, Philip, Bartholomew, Matthew, Thomas, James son of Alphaeus, Thaddaeus, Simon the Zealot and Judas Iscariot, who betrayed him.

The twelve men Jesus asked to be his apostles could have offered lots of reasons why they were not fit to serve. They were common men with no special standing in the eyes of the world. Yet when Jesus called, they came—fishermen, tax collectors and even revolutionaries. History shows that their faith and obedience to Jesus Christ changed the world profoundly.

When Jesus calls us to follow him, he's not looking for the smartest or the strongest or the bravest. He doesn't check our résumé or call our list of references. Scripture is full of stories of men and women who were used powerfully by God despite their lack of experience or expertise. How about you? Is God asking you to accept an assignment that seems far beyond your comfort zone? Are you afraid that you might fail? Are you afraid that you might succeed?

Take heart from this account of those Jesus chose to be his closest companions—those who would carry on his work. They changed the world not because of what they had in themselves but because of the One who empowered them. And they were part of something wonderful.

On the plains of Moab by the Jordan across from Jericho the LORD said to Moses, "Speak to the Israelites and say to them: 'When you cross the Jordan into Canaan, drive out all the inhabitants of the land before you. Destroy all their carved images and their cast idols, and demolish all their high places. Take possession of the land and settle in it, for I have given you the land to possess. Distribute the land by lot, according to your clans. To a larger group give a larger inheritance, and to a smaller group a smaller one. Whatever falls to them by lot will be theirs. Distribute it according to your ancestral tribes.

"'But if you do not drive out the inhabitants of the land, those you allow to remain will become barbs in your eyes and thorns in your sides. They will give you trouble in the land where you will live. And then I will do to you what I plan to do to them.' "

I magine the excitement of the Israelites who, after a 40-year journey, were finally preparing to enter the land long promised to them by God. God had led them through the desert and now everything was culminating in the final conquest. On the eve of this momentous invasion came a sobering message from God that when his people took possession of the land they were to run off the inhabitants and destroy their religious symbols.

Why would God utter such harsh words and follow them up with a harsh warning in the middle of all the joy and excitement? The answer is simple: The Israelites' emotional excitement about moving into the promised land had made them nearsighted. They weren't thinking about ensuring their longevity and blessings in the beautiful land. They weren't thinking that far ahead.

God remained farsighted, however. And what he saw made him warn his children about the dangers that could have devastating effects on their devotion to him. God is similarly farsighted on our behalf when it comes to marriage. When we join God in taking the long view of our marriage, we begin to see that amidst the excitement and joy of wedding festivities, we have a serious calling. We must meet any stumbling blocks to marriage—and meet them head-on and with faith that God will show us the way.

When Mephibosheth son of Jonathan, the son of Saul, came to David, he bowed down to pay him honor.

David said, "Mephibosheth!"

"Your servant," he replied.

"Don't be afraid," David said to him, "for I will surely show you kindness for the sake of your father Jonathan. I will restore to you all the land that belonged to your grandfather Saul, and you will always eat at my table."

Mephibosheth bowed down and said, "What is your servant, that you should notice a dead dog like me?"

Then the king summoned Ziba, Saul's servant, and said to him, "I have given your master's grandson everything that belonged to Saul and his family. You and your sons and your servants are to farm the land for him and bring in the crops, so that your master's grandson may be provided for. And Mephibosheth, grandson of your master, will always eat at my table." (Now Ziba had fifteen sons and twenty servants.)

Then Ziba said to the king, "Your servant will do whatever my lord the king commands his servant to do." So Mephibosheth ate at David's table like one of the king's sons.

Many years after his friend Jonathan died, King David reached out to Jonathan's son Mephibosheth. David restored to Mephibosheth the land that had belonged to his grandfather, King Saul, and David welcomed Mephibosheth to his royal table. Why? Because David loved Jonathan and wanted to do something kind to a member of Saul's household "for Jonathan's sake."

Sometimes we don't want to extend ourselves on behalf of anyone else. But when two people marry they don't become involved with just one other person. Spouses come with a constellation of family and friends. We can ignore those relationships. We can view them as a threat to our relationship with our spouse and fight them. Or we can lovingly insert ourselves into those other relationships and help grow them.

We don't have to develop intimate friendships with all of our spouse's relatives and close friends. But as David understood, we can best honor, love and serve our spouse, by making loving overtures to the people he or she loves.

Daniel 3:16-23

Shadrach, Meshach and Abednego replied to the king, "O Nebuchadnezzar, we do not need to defend ourselves before you in this matter. If we are thrown into the blazing furnace, the God we serve is able to save us from it, and he will rescue us from your hand, O king. But even if he does not, we want you to know, O king, that we will not serve your gods or worship the image of gold you have set up."

Then Nebuchadnezzar was furious with Shadrach, Meshach and Abednego, and his attitude toward them changed. He ordered the furnace heated seven times hotter than usual and commanded some of the strongest soldiers in his army to tie up Shadrach, Meshach and Abednego and throw them into the blazing furnace. So these men, wearing their robes, trousers, turbans and other clothes, were bound and thrown into the blazing furnace. The king's command was so urgent and the furnace so hot that the flames of the fire killed the soldiers who took up Shadrach, Meshach and Abednego, and these three men, firmly tied, fell into the blazing furnace.

Shadrach, Meshach and Abednego survived a close encounter with martyrdom. Because they defied the ruling authorities they were scheduled to be thrown into a furnace. But trusting God to honor their faithfulness, they vowed fidelity—even if it cost them their lives. While we know the end of the story (they lived), they had no certainty that they would survive the raging blaze when they stood up for God. And though they were certain of God's power and willingness to protect them, they didn't demand that he save them.

Many Christians face persecution today. At some point many more will have to make the choice to denounce God or risk everything they hold dear, including their lives. And many face such choices now, though with less-threatening consequences. For example, we may be ostracized from our families or passed over for promotions. We may be treated unjustly or misunderstood.

Have you ever thought about what you would do if you were faced with dire persecution? Are you willing to risk everything because you are convinced that loving God is worth whatever sacrifices you face? When faced with the choice to remain faithful, think of the three young men in Babylon who counted their own lives as nothing compared to the grace they had been given.

Lamentations 3:21-32

Yet this I call to mind and therefore I have hope:
Because of the LORD's great love we are not consumed,
for his compassions never fail.
They are new every morning; great is your faithfulness.
I say to myself, "The LORD is my portion; therefore I will wait for him."
The LORD is good to those whose hope is in him, to the one who seeks him;
it is good to wait quietly for the salvation of the LORD.
It is good for a man to bear the yoke while he is young.
Let him sit alone in silence, for the LORD has laid it on him.
Let him bury his face in the dust—there may yet be hope.
Let him offer his cheek to one who would strike him,
and let him be filled with disgrace.
For men are not cast off by the Lord forever.
Though he brings grief, he will show compassion,
so great is his unfailing love.

A fresh start

In the book of Lamentations, the prophet Jeremiah looks back at the destruction of Jerusalem. God promised that his people would face punishment for their sinful choices, and he was true to his word. Their city had been ravaged, and they were now living in exile.

In the midst of Jeremiah's lament, however, he remembers God's mercy. Were it not for that mercy, every one of God's people would have perished. The judgment on them was painful, but God would not leave them ruined.

Maybe you have experienced the discipline of God in your own life. You have suffered painful consequences for sinful choices you have made. Perhaps you feel that God has left you there. If so, remember that although God is just, he is also full of mercy. His compassions never fail. He promises to forgive us when we come to him and confess what we have done or not done. No matter how you have offended God, you can have hope because of his great mercy. You can always have a fresh start with him because his compassions are "new every morning." So take some time to thank God for the specific ways he has acted mercifully toward you.

Mark 8:34-38

*Then he called the crowd to him
along with his disciples and said: "If
anyone would come after me, he
must deny himself and take up his
cross and follow me. For whoever
wants to save his life will lose it, but
whoever loses his life for me and
for the gospel will save it. What
good is it for a man to gain the
whole world, yet forfeit his soul? Or
what can a man give in exchange
for his soul? If anyone is ashamed
of me and my words in this
adulterous and sinful generation,
the Son of Man will be ashamed of
him when he comes in his
Father's glory with the holy angels."*

In Mark 8 Jesus not only challenges us to relinquish earthly treasures and comforts but to go one step further—to deny ourselves. Deny your interests, wants and desires. Be willing to deny even safety and self-protection. Be willing to lose your very life for me, Jesus said.

Living out Christ-like self-denial is hard enough to do with friends, family members and acquaintances. But it's even tougher in the intimate, day-to-day interactions of marriage. Preoccupation with self is our default mode, and when things don't go our way, we immediately start wondering, "What about my feelings? My wants? My dreams? My hopes? My hurts?"

Self-denial in marriage can be as simple as going to the restaurant your spouse likes even though it's not your favorite, turning off the big game to have some couple time, or keeping an opinion to yourself to prevent unnecessary conflict. Or it can be as tough as putting your career on hold so your spouse can take his or her dream job, opening up about painful issues that you'd prefer to bury, or waiting to have children because your spouse isn't ready. Yes, denying ourselves isn't easy, but it often leads to a better way of living and loving.

Jeremiah 15:18-21

Why is my pain unending
    and my wound grievous and
        incurable?
Will you be to me like a
    deceptive brook,
like a spring that fails?

Therefore this is what the
    LORD says:
    "If you repent, I will restore you
    that you may serve me;
    if you utter worthy, not
        worthless, words,
    you will be my spokesman.
    Let this people turn to you,
    but you must not turn to them.

I will make you a wall to this people,
    a fortified wall of bronze;
    they will fight against you
    but will not overcome you,
    for I am with you
    to rescue and save you,"
    declares the LORD.

"I will save you from the hands of
    the wicked
    and redeem you from
    the grasp of the cruel."

B eing a prophet was certainly the most discouraging job on earth. However that doesn't mean that God is a cosmic taskmaster who doles out difficult assignments to teach people like Jeremiah to trust him more. Instead, God gave Jeremiah the freedom to express his doubts. Jeremiah did so on several occasions, and the audacity in his words reveals his intimacy with God.

In turn, the Lord responded with firm grace: "If you repent I will restore you that you may serve me." In other words, there is a time to express doubt, but there is also a point at which we must return to our senses before we forget who God is and what he's called us to do. Talk to God about your doubts and your questions, but don't go so far that you begin to lose focus of who you are and who God is.

Are you in the middle of a seemingly impossible assignment? Are you wondering if God really knows how much you can take? God knows your limits. He realizes that he calls flawed people to enormous tasks. Yet his promise is forever the same: "I am with you always, to the very end of the age" (Matthew 28:20).

Caleb said, "I was forty years old when Moses the servant of the LORD sent me from Kadesh Barnea to explore the land. And I brought him back a report according to my convictions, but my brothers who went up with me made the hearts of the people melt with fear. I, however, followed the LORD my God wholeheartedly. So on that day Moses swore to me, 'The land on which your feet have walked will be your inheritance and that of your children forever, because you have followed the LORD my God wholeheartedly.'

"Now then, just as the LORD promised, he has kept me alive for forty-five years since the time he said this to Moses, while Israel moved about in the desert. So here I am today, eighty-five years old! I am still as strong today as the day Moses sent me out; I'm just as vigorous to go out to battle now as I was then. Now give me this hill country that the LORD promised me that day." Then Joshua blessed Caleb son of Jephunneh and gave him Hebron as his inheritance.

When we marry, we make promises to one another. But we also depend on the promises God makes about marriage. Just as God promised Caleb that he would get an inheritance, God promises Christians that he will bless their marriages. Some couples wait a long time to experience the fulfillment of that promise. And many marriages seem to have so much wrong with them.

When you and your spouse experience conflict, emptiness, dissatisfaction or hopelessness in your marriage, it's time to remember God's promises. He doesn't do things on our timetable; he does them on his own. Because he is a perfect God, his timetable is perfect.

Caleb understood that. He forthrightly reminded God of his promise and explained how he had been faithful to God when most of the other spies had not been. Caleb did not doubt that God would do what he had promised. And guess what? God was faithful; he gave Hebron to Caleb.

The LORD appeared to Solomon during the night in a dream, and God said, "Ask for whatever you want me to give you."

"Now, O LORD my God, you have made your servant king in place of my father David," Solomon said. "But I am only a little child and do not know how to carry out my duties. Your servant is here among the people you have chosen, a great people, too numerous to count or number. Give your servant a discerning heart to govern your people and to distinguish between right and wrong."

The Lord was pleased that Solomon had asked for this. God said to him, "… I will do what you have asked. I will give you a wise and discerning heart, so that there will never have been anyone like you, nor will there ever be. Moreover, I will give you what you have not asked for—both riches and honor—so that in your lifetime you will have no equal among kings." …

Then Solomon awoke—and he realized it had been a dream. He returned to Jerusalem, stood before the ark of the Lord's covenant and sacrificed burnt offerings and fellowship offerings.

Worship and wisdom

Worship is like the rains that prepare the earth for God's blessings. The story of the youthful Solomon preparing to take the throne is a beautiful reminder to us of the importance of worship. The story of God granting him the gift of wisdom opens with a swell of costly and reverent worship. For us, too, worship creates a context for us to encounter God; it sets our souls in motion in an upward spiral by which we pursue God, and he gladly responds.

Worship book-ended the exchange between the Sovereign God and the new sovereign of Israel. Solomon returned from his heavenly encounter and again made an offering to the God of Israel in Jerusalem before the ark of the covenant.

Like a gathering cloud, worship encircles and protects God's people. It softens the soil of our hearts like nourishing rain. When we've been in a dark place and long for colorful beauty to replace the hardness that has settled into our scorched souls, simple acts of worship can prepare the way for God's words of wisdom to permeate our hearts. If your life seems parched, won't you allow God to paint a palette of colorful joy by spending time worshipping your Lord?

1 Corinthians 13:1-8, 13

If I speak in the tongues of men and of angels, but have not love, I am only a resounding gong or a clanging cymbal. If I have the gift of prophecy and can fathom all mysteries and all knowledge, and if I have a faith that can move mountains, but have not love, I am nothing. If I give all I possess to the poor and surrender my body to the flames, but have not love, I gain nothing.

Love is patient, love is kind. It does not envy, it does not boast, it is not proud. It is not rude, it is not self-seeking, it is not easily angered, it keeps no record of wrongs. Love does not delight in evil but rejoices with the truth. It always protects, always trusts, always hopes, always perseveres.

Love never fails. But where there are prophecies, they will cease; where there are tongues, they will be stilled; where there is knowledge, it will pass away. …

And now these three remain: faith, hope and love. But the greatest of these is love.

One-hit wonderful

In the music industry, a one-hit wonder is a musician famous for one smash hit. Their tunes are faddish and their popularity short-lived. In 1 Corinthians 13:1-3, Paul listed some attributes that fall into the great, but not greatest, category of one-hit wonders known to human beings: faith and hope. But nothing can compete with the greatest attribute of all: love. In God's book, love is one-hit wonderful. If you're going to be known for anything, let it be love. Your lifelong goal should be to embody the diverse characteristics of love found in 1 Corinthians 13.

Unfortunately, the English language is limited to only one word to describe the many types of love. As a result, our understanding of genuine love is inadequate; we tend to confuse one kind with another. The Greek language, however, has several words for love, such as *eros*, meaning romantic love, and *philia*, or friendship. But Paul used the Greek word *agape* to describe love that is divine; this type of love originates with God. It is eternal; it never fails.

Live today seeking the greatest of all attributes. Try to express the heart of biblical love in all that you say and do. Let today be your love song, your one-hit wonderful to everyone you encounter.

Genesis 32:22-30

That night Jacob got up and took his two wives, his two maidservants and his eleven sons and crossed the ford of the Jabbok. After he had sent them across the stream, he sent over all his possessions. So Jacob was left alone, and a man wrestled with him till daybreak. When the man saw that he could not overpower him, he touched the socket of Jacob's hip so that his hip was wrenched as he wrestled with the man. Then the man said, "Let me go, for it is daybreak." But Jacob replied, "I will not let you go unless you bless me."

The man asked him, "What is your name?"
"Jacob," he answered.

Then the man said, "Your name will no longer be Jacob, but Israel, because you have struggled with God and with men and have overcome."

Jacob said, "Please tell me your name."
But he replied, "Why do you ask my name?" Then he blessed him there.

So Jacob called the place Peniel, saying, "It is because I saw God face to face, and yet my life was spared."

There's a good reason God calls his people sheep. Sometimes they act ba-a-a-ad and wander away from the paths he has mapped out for them. A good shepherd will relentlessly search for a wayward sheep. Sometimes, if the sheep refuses to follow his master, the shepherd takes drastic action. He breaks the sheep's leg, places it upon his shoulders and carries the sheep until it learns total dependence.

God wanted to make Jacob into a different person, so he took drastic action. He initiated a wrestling match that lasted from dusk till dawn. Jacob's willfulness would not allow him to give up. So the man "broke" Jacob, touching his hip so that he walked with a limp for the rest of his life. Many people might become bitter and turn away from God for breaking them. But Jacob had just the opposite response. He clung to God saying, "I will not let you go unless you bless me."

We may think that a God of love would never allow his children to feel any pain. But sometimes God breaks us to make us better. Like Jacob, the best response to God's tough love is to cling to him and earnestly pray, "I will not let you go unless you bless me."

Leviticus 19:33-34

When an alien lives with you in your land, do not mistreat him. The alien living with you must be treated as one of your native-born. Love him as yourself, for you were aliens in Egypt. I am the Lord your God.

ildred Hoyt, "Mid" to her friends, left this world and went to rest in the arms of Jesus at the age of ninety-seven. She was born December 24, 1899. Imagine what her eyes saw, the changes that transformed this world of ours—it's staggering if you think about it. Spending time with Mid left one with a longing—a longing to return to a different time. A time of simplicity, a time for family and community.

Perhaps a similar longing prompted a group of so-called aliens to accompany the Israelites out of Egypt. These aliens just didn't fit in Egypt anymore. They longed for a life that honored God. They had seen God's power and wanted what he offered. God honored their determination by protecting them with this commandment, reminding the Israelites that they, too, had once been aliens in a foreign land.

Who are the aliens today? Perhaps the alien is a neighbor who admires your faith and with a little encouragement would come to church with you. Perhaps the alien is someone at work whose lifestyle you would not choose, but who might be drawn to God through your gracious attitude. The challenge is to live the Golden Rule in the desert of life. Don't greet the aliens as strangers, but treat them as you would one of your friends or family. Treat the aliens in your life to a taste of God's love.

Sing to the LORD, all the earth;
proclaim his salvation day after day.

Declare his glory among
the nations, his marvelous
deeds among all peoples.

For great is the LORD and
most worthy of praise; he is
to be feared above all gods.

For all the gods of the na-
tions are idols, but the LORD
made the heavens.

Splendor and majesty are
before him; strength and
joy in his dwelling place.

Ascribe to the LORD, O fami-
lies of nations, ascribe to the
LORD glory and strength,

ascribe to the LORD the glory due
his name. Bring an offering and
come before him; worship the LORD
in the splendor of his holiness.

Tremble before him, all the
earth! The world is firmly estab-
lished; it cannot be moved.

Let the heavens rejoice, let the
earth be glad; let them say among
the nations, "The LORD reigns!"

Let the sea resound, and all that
is in it; let the fields be jubi-
lant, and everything in them!

Then the trees of the forest will sing,
they will sing for joy before the LORD,
for he comes to judge the earth.

Give thanks to the LORD, for he is
good; his love endures forever.

Even deeper than gratitude for a favor or thankfulness in the midst of misery, thanksgiving can be viewed as a testament to an enduring quality in someone we admire and respect. For instance, David celebrated God's divine attributes with a heart of pure thanksgiving. With great fanfare, the ark of the covenant had finally arrived in Jerusalem and taken its place in the tent David had prepared for it. After the offerings were made and the feast was over, David's gladness spilled over into a great song of jubilant thanksgiving.

Consider the countless reasons you have to be grateful. Has something brought great joy to your life? Consider the attributes of those you love: your husband's faithfulness, your friends' trustworthiness, your parents' goodness, your child's tender heart.

Today is the perfect time to "give thanks to the Lord, for he is good." Start by expressing thanks for some of the things David included in his prayer: wonderful acts, miracles, salvation, glory, marvelous deeds among all peoples, holiness. Everything about God is worthy of our praise. Let us not allow anyone or anything to rob us of the gift of a thankful heart.

John 13:2-5, 12-16

The evening meal was being served, and the devil had already prompted Judas Iscariot, son of Simon, to betray Jesus. Jesus knew that the Father had put all things under his power, and that he had come from God and was returning to God; so he got up from the meal, took off his outer clothing, and wrapped a towel around his waist. After that, he poured water into a basin and began to wash his disciples' feet, drying them with the towel that was wrapped around him. …

When he had finished washing their feet, he put on his clothes and returned to his place. "Do you understand what I have done for you?" he asked them. "You call me 'Teacher' and 'Lord,' and rightly so, for that is what I am. Now that I, your Lord and Teacher, have washed your feet, you also should wash one another's feet. I have set you an example that you should do as I have done for you. I tell you the truth, no servant is greater than his master, nor is a messenger greater than the one who sent him."

Servant leaders

Jesus was the ultimate servant leader. He knew he would be putting his mission in the hands of the disciples in the coming hours as he headed to the cross. It would soon be their turn to spread the Good News of the gospel message. So he demonstrated servant leadership in a profoundly beautiful way. On the night before his trial and crucifixion, Jesus took the lead by humbly, lovingly kneeling at the feet of his followers and washing the dirt from their feet.

Perhaps he was thinking of how their feet would carry them to parts of the world they probably hadn't even yet heard about as they spread the Good News about the Messiah. Perhaps he prayed that their feet would stand strong when they faced the persecution to come. This was surely a precious, intimate moment with his friends.

We women have grown accustomed to serving our friends and family. We serve dinner and wash dishes. We wash dirty faces. We wash loads and loads of laundry. As we carry out our roles as servants, may we humbly lead those we love to the servant leader Jesus, the One who was willing to humble himself and wash us "whiter than snow" (Psalm 51:7).

Whenever they saw that there was a large amount of money in the chest, the royal secretary and the high priest came, counted the money that had been brought into the temple of the Lᴏʀᴅ and put it into bags. When the amount had been determined, they gave the money to the men appointed to supervise the work on the temple. With it they paid those who worked on the temple of the Lᴏʀᴅ—the carpenters and builders, the masons and stonecutters. They purchased timber and dressed stone for the repair of the temple of the Lᴏʀᴅ, and met all the other expenses of restoring the temple.

The money brought into the temple was not spent for making silver basins, wick trimmers, sprinkling bowls, trumpets or any other articles of gold or silver for the temple of the Lᴏʀᴅ; it was paid to the workmen, who used it to repair the temple. They did not require an accounting from those to whom they gave the money to pay the workers, because they acted with complete honesty.

The truth will come out

The workers described in 2 Kings 12 realized the value of trustworthiness. They were so well known for their complete honesty that they weren't required to give an account for how they spent the vast amounts of money allotted for the temple's reconstruction.

How different that scene in 2 Kings is from the scene in Genesis 3, where God confronted Adam and Eve and demanded an accounting from them after their fateful encounter with the serpent. For the first time in this first couple's lives—which had been perfect, stress-free and marked by an ongoing, intimate relationship with their Creator—the two garden-dwellers were asked to account for their actions to God himself. Why? Because they had listened to the serpent's lies, compromised what they knew to be the truth of God's Word and allowed sin to invade paradise.

Can you relate? Maybe your lies don't seem serpent-sized, but even so-called white lies can open the door to compromise and sin. Wouldn't it be better to live like the straightforward workers in this story? Their reputation for "complete honesty" went before them, gaining them the respect of their superiors and even the king.

Job 38:1-13

*Then the L*ORD *answered Job out of the storm. He said:*
"Who is this that darkens my counsel with words without knowledge?
Brace yourself like a man; I will question you, and you shall answer me.
Where were you when I laid the earth's foundation?
Tell me, if you understand.
Who marked off its dimensions? Surely you know!
Who stretched a measuring line across it?
On what were its footings set, or who laid its cornerstone while the morning
stars sang together and all the angels shouted for joy?
Who shut up the sea behind doors when it burst forth from the womb,
when I made the clouds its garment and wrapped it in thick darkness, when
I fixed limits for it and set its doors and bars in place, when I said, 'This far
you may come and no farther; here is where your proud waves halt'?
Have you ever given orders to the morning, or shown the dawn its place,
that it might take the earth by the edges and shake the wicked out of it?"

For thirty-seven chapters Job and his friends have grappled with the question of suffering. Why do people suffer? Is it because God isn't there? Because God doesn't care? Because the one suffering has done something to displease God? Job and his friends have gone around and around and still come up empty. Finally God "answered Job out of the storm."

God didn't deign to tell Job the reason for Job's suffering, but he did remind Job that he is the mighty God who marked the dimensions of the earth, fixed the limits of the sea and blanketed the sky with clouds. This is the God whom Job and his friends dared to question. The audacity of trying to bring God down to their level! But when God spoke, he showed them how much bigger and more magnificent were his ways than their ways.

Have you been grappling with pain and suffering? Are you trying to figure out why God has allowed sorrow and trouble to come into your life? The best solution isn't to talk endlessly with your friends and try to figure out the reasons for your suffering. Wait for God to speak with you in the midst of the storm.

Ephesians 2:4-10

Because of his great love for us, God, who is rich in mercy, made us alive with Christ even when we were dead in transgressions—it is by grace you have been saved. And God raised us up with Christ and seated us with him in the heavenly realms in Christ Jesus, in order that in the coming ages he might show the incomparable riches of his grace, expressed in his kindness to us in Christ Jesus. For it is by grace you have been saved through faith—and this not from yourselves, it is the gift of God—not by works, so that no one can boast. For we are God's workmanship, created in Christ Jesus to do good works, which God prepared in advance for us to do.

W hat assignment has God given you? Would you ask Him? We know He has one in mind for you because He told us clearly through the words of the apostle Paul, that "we are God's workmanship, created in Christ Jesus to do good works, which God prepared in advance for us to do."

Don't dodge your assignment because it seems to lack any chance for success. Don't miss your assignment because it seems such an insignificant, small thing. The church in Europe was birthed when Paul spoke to a handful of women on a river bank. The size and scope of the assignment are up to him, and the effectiveness and lasting impact of your service are also his responsibility. We are simply to be faithfully available and obedient.

In the meantime, with eyes opened, heart rended and knees bent, whisper, "Yes ... Yes, Lord! ... Yes, Sir!" then raise your hand and say, "I'm available for service. Send me. I'll go."

Jacob's sons had come in from the fields as soon as they heard what had happened. They were filled with grief and fury, because Shechem had done a disgraceful thing in Israel by lying with Jacob's daughter. …

Jacob's sons replied deceitfully as they spoke to Shechem and his father Hamor. They said to them, "We can't do such a thing; we can't give our sister to a man who is not circumcised. That would be a disgrace to us. We will give our consent to you on one condition only: that you become like us by circumcising all your males. Then we will give you our daughters and take your daughters for ourselves. We'll settle among you and become one people with you. But if you will not agree to be circumcised, we'll take our sister and go."

Their proposal sounded good to Hamor and his son, Shechem. …

Three days later, while all of them were still in pain, two of Jacob's sons, Simeon and Levi, Dinah's brothers, took their swords and attacked the unsuspecting city, killing every male. … They carried off all their wealth and all their women and children, taking as plunder everything in the houses.

D inah was Jacob's only daughter. When she ventured from her family's home to visit with the local people, she was taken and raped by Shechem, the son of a local ruler.

No one is the same after sin—not the victim, not the perpetrator and not those who love the victim or victimizer. In this story, Shechem was a powerful man who thought he could have whatever he wanted. So he took it. Unfortunately, he paid the price with his life, and his men paid the price with their lives.

No one suffers or sins in a vacuum. We can see that in the results of sin all around us. But we can see it in our own lives too. Maybe you have been abused or taken advantage of. You may feel that you have no future or hope. Yet God can work through any situation. He cannot change the past, but he can work through your present to help you cope, change, grow and ultimately thrive. No matter what happened to you, God knows. Turn to him for comfort. Turn to him with your pain. Ask him to heal your hurting heart and restore you. He is the only one who can restore your soul.

Psalm 145:1, 3-6

I will exalt you, my God the King;
I will praise your name for ever and ever.

Great is the LORD and most worthy of praise;
his greatness no one can fathom.

One generation will commend your works to another;
they will tell of your mighty acts.

They will speak of the glorious
splendor of your majesty, and I will meditate on your wonderful works.

They will tell of the power of your awesome works,
and I will proclaim your great deeds.

God in your brag book

Whom do you brag about? Do your friends hear about your brilliant daughter, your generous sister, your adorable puppy? Have you in turn seen every photo of a friend's grandchild, heard about every new word, every tooth and every step?

How often do you brag about God? People in your life need to hear from you about him—your children, nieces and nephews, grandchildren, neighborhood kids, everyone. They will someday have their own stories of how their prayers were answered. They will learn about God's faithfulness as they go through hard times. God will bless them with delightful surprises. They will experience God's mercy and tenderness for themselves. But until they have their own stories, they need to hear yours. Your stories will "prime the pump" as it were and alert them to watch for God as they "live and move and have [their] being" in him (Acts 17:28).

It's easy to complain about inefficient checkout clerks, dangerous drivers and ungrateful relatives. But it's so much sweeter and deeper to bless others with stories about the good things we've experienced with God. It's so rewarding to look for opportunities to praise God and to remember how he has been good to us. It's so wonderfully fun to brag about God.

1 Peter 4:7-11

The end of all things is near. Therefore be clear minded and self-controlled so that you can pray. Above all, love each other deeply, because love covers over a multitude of sins. Offer hospitality to one another without grumbling. Each one should use whatever gift he has received to serve others, faithfully administering God's grace in its various forms. If anyone speaks, he should do it as one speaking the very words of God. If anyone serves, he should do it with the strength God provides, so that in all things God may be praised through Jesus Christ. To him be the glory and the power for ever and ever. Amen.

We tend to throw the word love around pretty casually. We send our spouses off to work with a casual "Love you," toss in a little affection during a midday phone conversation or e-mail, and offer a pleasant "Goodnight, I love you" before falling asleep. But what happens in between all those professions of love? Does the love you share with your spouse really "cover over a multitude of sins"?

For many of us, it doesn't. We nag each other, criticize each other, bicker with each other. We complain about the dirty socks he leaves on the floor or the crusty dishes she leaves in the sink. We snap at each other, belittle each other and take out our frustrations on each other. We find it almost impossible to ignore all the ways our spouse drives us crazy.

But when the love of God fills us, it flushes out selfishness, greed, disrespect and petty criticism. It's that deep love, the love that overrides our base instincts, that allows us to live well with our spouses.

David conferred with each of his officers, the commanders of thousands and commanders of hundreds. He then said to the whole assembly of Israel, "If it seems good to you and if it is the will of the LORD our God, let us send word far and wide to the rest of our brothers throughout the territories of Israel, and also to the priests and Levites who are with them in their towns and pasture-lands, to come and join us. Let us bring the ark of our God back to us, for we did not inquire of it during the reign of Saul." The whole assembly agreed to do this, because it seemed right to all the people.

So David assembled all the Israel-ites, from the Shihor River in Egypt to Lebo Hamath, to bring the ark of God from Kiriath Jearim. David and all the Israelites with him went to Baalah of Judah (Kiriath Jearim) to bring up from there the ark of God the LORD, who is enthroned between the cherubim—the ark that is called by the Name.

After David assumed the throne of Israel, he recognized that the people had been remiss in thinking about God. Their leader, King Saul, had been unfaithful to God and hadn't sought God's guidance for some time. So David's first royal act was to bring the ark of the covenant to Jerusalem, back to its place at the center of worship among the people of God as a physical reminder of God's presence, sovereignty and faithfulness. Physical reminders of God can help us take time to talk to him and to listen to him.

We are also reminded of God through his people. Take a moment to express your love and thanksgiving to God for encircling you with loving friends and family.

And if we develop eyes to see, God will give us glimpses of himself through the beauty of nature, a blooming rose bush, a glorious sunset, a soft snowfall. Take time to whisper a prayer of adoration. You can also place reminders around your home or office to trigger thoughts of God: your favorite Bible sitting by the chair; books, music and artwork placed in prominent positions. Don't let a day go by after which you wonder, "Did I think about God today?"

David said to Abigail, "Praise be to the L<small>ORD</small>, the God of Israel, who has sent you today to meet me. May you be blessed for your good judgment and for keeping me from bloodshed this day and from avenging myself with my own hands. Otherwise, as surely as the L<small>ORD</small>, the God of Israel, lives, who has kept me from harming you, if you had not come quickly to meet me, not one male belonging to Nabal would have been left alive by daybreak."

ailure to return hospitality carried serious implications in biblical times. Foolish, alcohol-abusing Nabal had insulted David by refusing to offer him and his men the typical Eastern courtesy: a share in the bounty of his household at sheep-shearing time. In so doing, Nabal put his wife and entire household at risk of retaliation. When Abigail heard about the situation, she could have responded by criticizing her husband or cursing his stupidity. She did neither. She restored peace on behalf of her household. Her discernment and tact calmed David's anger and honored God.

Abigail offered hospitality in the face of hostility. David was grateful that her wise intervention stopped him from committing murder.

While your community may not punish rudeness or slander with actual warfare, you're probably very familiar with the damage that smoldering hostility or gossip can bring to a family, a workplace or a church. When you become aware of an escalating crisis, ask God to give you the discernment to think quickly and act decisively. Then intervene with kindness on your lips and grace in your heart. Like Abigail, use the resources that God has placed at your disposal to help find a peaceful solution to a possibly explosive situation.

On the plains of Moab by the Jordan across from Jericho the LORD said to Moses, "Speak to the Israelites and say to them: 'When you cross the Jordan into Canaan, drive out all the inhabitants of the land before you. Destroy all their carved images and their cast idols, and demolish all their high places. Take possession of the land and settle in it, for I have given you the land to possess. Distribute the land by lot, according to your clans. To a larger group give a larger inheritance, and to a smaller group a smaller one. Whatever falls to them by lot will be theirs. Distribute it according to your ancestral tribes.

" 'But if you do not drive out the inhabitants of the land, those you allow to remain will become barbs in your eyes and thorns in your sides. They will give you trouble in the land where you will live. And then I will do to you what I plan to do to them.' "

No loopholes

Can you hear the Israelites' thoughts as they finally entered the promised land? God tells them to drive everyone from the land. Every single person living in the land has got to go. Wait a minute! How could our good and loving God drive these folks from their homes? Even fragile women, helpless old people and innocent little children? That's just not fair! Sometimes we come to portions of the Bible we cannot reconcile with our notions of what is fair.

God is loving and fair. But God is also just. God recognized that the Canaanites were thoroughly infected with the highly contagious disease of idolatry. Allowing them to stay in the land would mean exposing the Israelites to their contamination. The moral illness would certainly destroy them.

Do you ever find yourself second-guessing God? Even after his instruction is clearly laid out in his Word? God doesn't ask for our advice or our input—just our obedience, even when his ways don't seem to make sense. The truth is this: There is no better way than God's way in every area, in all things, at all times. God is good and loving and just. And he always, in all ways, knows best.

John 17:8-13

"I gave them the words you gave me and they accepted them. They knew with certainty that I came from you, and they believed that you sent me. I pray for them. I am not praying for the world, but for those you have given me, for they are yours. All I have is yours, and all you have is mine. And glory has come to me through them. I will remain in the world no longer, but they are still in the world, and I am coming to you. Holy Father, protect them by the power of your name—the name you gave me—so that they may be one as we are one. While I was with them, I protected them and kept them safe by that name you gave me. None has been lost except the one doomed to destruction so that Scripture would be fulfilled. I am coming to you now, but I say these things while I am still in the world, so that they may have the full measure of my joy within them."

Full of joy

In his final prayer, Jesus prayed that his disciples would experience the full measure of his joy—now. He prayed for us to have his joy in the middle of rush-hour traffic, screaming kids and a darkening world. He doesn't want us to wait for heaven to be full of joy.

Jesus' joy has a divine purpose: to reveal him. He desires to fill us with overflowing joy, to proclaim his victory to the world over life's worst conditions—even in the face of hurricanes, plagues, terrorism and nuclear disaster.

But joy flows from a foundation of truth. So many times we focus on imaginary troubles. But Jesus reminds us that joy comes from knowing the Father through the Son. As you reflect on your life, whether you're eighteen or eighty-eight, choose to live in fullness of joy by taking the time to pick more daisies—and by living each moment fully aware of God's love for you.

When the queen of Sheba heard about the fame of Solomon and his relation to the name of the LORD, she came to test him with hard questions. Arriving at Jerusalem with a very great caravan—with camels carrying spices, large quantities of gold, and precious stones—she came to Solomon and talked with him about all that she had on her mind. Solomon answered all her questions; nothing was too hard for the king to explain to her. When the queen of Sheba saw all the wisdom of Solomon and the palace he had built, the food on his table, the seating of his officials, the attending servants in their robes, his cupbearers, and the burnt offerings he made at the temple of the LORD, she was overwhelmed.

She said to the king, "The report I heard in my own country about your achievements and your wisdom is true. But I did not believe these things until I came and saw with my own eyes. Indeed, not even half was told me; in wisdom and wealth you have far exceeded the report I heard."

Life's questions

The Queen of Sheba had questions. And she didn't think twice about traveling 1500 miles to get answers. Over the years, her wise, elderly subjects often told her that the longer she lived, the more mysterious life would seem. All she knew was that she'd already lived long enough and seen enough of the world to have questions—lots of them. Why does poverty exist? Why do the innocent suffer? What is the meaning of life? Is this all there is?

She came to Jerusalem with much on her mind, determined to leave with a sense of satisfaction. And Solomon did not disappoint. To her delight, not only did Solomon answer all of her questions, he also explained them in a way that made sense to her.

"Naturally," she would later tell her people back home, "there were some questions Solomon didn't have to answer. 'Was the God of Israel as great as he claimed? Does he really bless those who serve him? Is there no end to his resources and might?' " The evidence, she concluded, spoke for itself. She merely had to look around for the answers.

We all have many questions. Ask God to grant you the wisdom to see his truth all around you.

Now Naaman was commander of the army of the king of Aram. He was a great man in the sight of his master and highly regarded, because through him the L‍ord had given victory to Aram. He was a valiant soldier, but he had leprosy.

Now bands from Aram had gone out and had taken captive a young girl from Israel, and she served Naaman's wife. She said to her mistress, "If only my master would see the prophet who is in Samaria! He would cure him of his leprosy."

I s your life happy except for one thing? Naaman, the commander, also experienced some significant excepts. He had great authority and was highly regarded by the king. Although he was a Gentile, he found favor with the God of Israel and was granted military victory. Except one thing plagued him: leprosy. If only he could find a cure, his life would be complete.

The slave girl and Naaman had choices to make concerning life's exceptions. Would they let the exceptions rule their lives? Or would they let God rule without exception? The slave girl could have let her situation make her bitter. Instead, she chose to help the man who was her master. And Naaman chose to take the advice of a servant girl, not allowing his pride to stand in the way of her help.

Is God asking you to take one step of obedience that may bring help and healing to another person? Perhaps it's as simple as taking up a pen and beginning a note of apology even though you're still hurting from what they did to you. Maybe you need to carve out time for the one thing you've been dreading to do. That first step of obedience can bring your exception into a different light when you learn step by step what it means to trust God without exceptions.

Then I saw a Lamb, looking as if it had been slain, standing in the center of the throne, encircled by the four living creatures and the elders. He had seven horns and seven eyes, which are the seven spirits of God sent out into all the earth. He came and took the scroll from the right hand of him who sat on the throne. And when he had taken it, the four living creatures and the twenty-four elders fell down before the Lamb. Each one had a harp and they were holding golden bowls full of incense, which are the prayers of the saints. And they sang a new song:

*"You are worthy to take the scroll
    and to open its seals,
    because you were slain,
    and with your blood you
    purchased men for God
     from every tribe and language
    and people and nation.
You have made them to be a
    kingdom and priests
    to serve our God, and
    they will reign on the earth."*

Once and for all

So much of our lives are spent trying to prove we are worthy—worthy of love, worthy of appreciation, worthy of value. The truth, especially for women, is that we battle feelings of unworthiness as followers of Jesus, as leaders, as mothers, as students, as neighbors. The truth is that we can never prove we're worthy because in and of ourselves we're not. In Revelation 5 John cried out with great weeping at the realization that no one in heaven, on earth, or under the earth was worthy to open the heavenly scroll.

Yet suddenly before John's eyes stood the only One worthy to open the scroll. By his blood—not by the blood, sweat and tears of our striving—we have been redeemed. We no longer have to prove our significance or earn our way. God has established our worth for all time.

In the light of eternity, it's good to know that your to-do list, the title on your business card, your clothing size, car or accomplishments have no bearing upon your worth. You have been made worthy not because of what you have or have not done, but because of what Jesus Christ has done on your behalf.

Isaiah 6:1-8

I saw the Lord seated on a throne, high and exalted, and the train of his robe filled the temple. Above him were seraphs, each with six wings: With two wings they covered their faces, with two they covered their feet, and with two they were flying. And they were calling to one another:

> *"Holy, holy, holy is the LORD Almighty;*
> *the whole earth is full of his glory."*

At the sound of their voices the doorposts and thresholds shook and the temple was filled with smoke.

"Woe to me!" I cried. "I am ruined! For I am a man of unclean lips, and I live among a people of unclean lips, and my eyes have seen the King, the LORD Almighty."

Then one of the seraphs flew to me with a live coal in his hand, which he had taken with tongs from the altar. With it he touched my mouth and said, "See, this has touched your lips; your guilt is taken away and your sin atoned for."

Then I heard the voice of the Lord saying, "Whom shall I send? And who will go for us?"

> *And I said, "Here am I. Send me!"*

The Israelites were in a mess—again. They were suffering because of their sinful ways. The problem was so immense and overwhelming that no one seemed able or even available to help.

God himself asked the question, "Whom shall I send? And who will go for us?" Isaiah answered, "Here am I. Send me!" What made Isaiah run to the problem rather than following the instinct to avoid conflict and personal danger? What prompted Isaiah to step forward and offer himself to God was an experience in worship that altered him forever. Everything pointed the prophet beyond the current task to the eternal glory of God. The weight of coming face-to-face with God was so intense that it nearly crushed Isaiah. Yet at the same time it revived and rejuvenated him. Seeing God in all his glory and splendor and worshipping him equipped Isaiah to serve God.

Like Isaiah, we can face hard assignments with confidence that if God has called us, he will equip us. Has God called you to a task for which you feel completely inadequate? The key to taking on the extraordinary challenge is to worship God. To spend time in his presence meditating on just how awesome he is.

In the course of time, Nahash king of the Ammonites died, and his son succeeded him as king. David thought, "I will show kindness to Hanun son of Nahash, because his father showed kindness to me." So David sent a delegation to express his sympathy to Hanun concerning his father.

When David's men came to Hanun in the land of the Ammonites to express sympathy to him, the Ammonite nobles said to Hanun, "Do you think David is honoring your father by sending men to you to express sympathy? Haven't his men come to you to explore and spy out the country and overthrow it?" So Hanun seized David's men, shaved them, cut off their garments in the middle at the buttocks, and sent them away.

When someone came and told David about the men, he sent messengers to meet them, for they were greatly humiliated.

ahash, the Ammonite king, had rendered some memorable service to King David. When he died, David responded by acting kindly toward Hanun, Nahash's son. However, David's kindness was misinterpreted. The men sent by David to express sympathy over Nahash's death were humiliated and accused of spying. War ensued, though it was certainly not the intended outcome of David's gesture.

Just as God unreservedly extends kindness to us, we are called to "clothe {ourselves} with compassion, kindness, humility, gentleness and patience." (Colossians 3:12). We are to reflect God's kindness to others, regardless of how they choose to respond.

Don't wait for a crisis to extend loving-kindness. Take the time to ponder who is suffering from a recent heartbreak. Maybe they could use a listening ear or a shoulder to cry on. Who feels discouraged in your circle of friends? Maybe they need to hear an encouraging word. Who might feel alone? Perhaps you could pick up the phone and tell them that you care ... and then leave the outcome to God.

Luke 8:22-27, 32-33

One day Jesus said to his disciples, "Let's go over to the other side of the lake." So they got into a boat and set out. As they sailed, he fell asleep. A squall came down on the lake, so that the boat was being swamped, and they were in great danger.

The disciples went and woke him, saying, "Master, Master, we're going to drown!"

He got up and rebuked the wind and the raging waters; the storm subsided, and all was calm. "Where is your faith?" he asked his disciples. In fear and amazement they asked one another, "Who is this? He commands even the winds and the water, and they obey him."

They sailed to the region of the Gerasenes, which is across the lake from Galilee. When Jesus stepped ashore, he was met by a demon-possessed man from the town.

A large herd of pigs was feeding there on the hillside. The demons begged Jesus to let them go into them, and he gave them permission. When the demons came out of the man, they went into the pigs, and the pigs rushed down the steep bank into the lake and were drowned.

As the disciples traveled with Jesus, there were a few surprises along the way. First, Jesus had turned water into wine at a wedding. Then he started healing people. Those healings were startling, clearly miraculous. Still, the disciples needed to see a miracle that hit them closer to home. When their friend and master stilled the angry sea with a single word, they were amazed and afraid. Suddenly, it wasn't the waves that were so intimidating, but the man in the boat with them who commanded the waves.

As they continued their travels with Jesus, they would need to know that he was more than a man, that he was the Christ. They would need this awareness as they stepped ashore after their traumatic boat trip because when they reached the shore, there were no banners saying "Welcome, Jesus and Friends." No, their welcoming committee was a screaming, naked man who lived among the tombs. The demons within this poor man knew who Jesus was and feared him. Perhaps now, after experiencing his power to save them and calm the elements, the disciples feared the demons less because they had grown to trust Jesus more personally than ever before.

Nehemiah 1:5-11

"O Lᴏʀᴅ, God of heaven, the great and awesome God, who keeps his covenant of love with those who love him and obey his commands, let your ear be attentive and your eyes open to hear the prayer your servant is praying before you day and night for your servants, the people of Israel. I confess the sins we Israelites, including myself and my father's house, have committed against you. We have acted very wickedly toward you.

"Remember the instruction you gave your servant Moses, saying, 'If you are unfaithful, I will scatter you among the nations, but if you return to me and obey my commands, then even if your exiled people are at the farthest horizon, I will gather them from there and bring them to the place I have chosen as a dwelling for my Name.'

"They are your servants and your people, whom you redeemed by your great strength and your mighty hand. O Lord, let your ear be attentive to the prayer of this your servant and to the prayer of your servants who delight in revering your name. Give your servant success today by granting him favor in the presence of this man."

A pattern for prayer

Nehemiah, one of the most powerful Jews in Babylon, broke down in tears when he heard of Jerusalem's miserable condition. He mourned for God's holy city and scattered people. His compassion compelled him to pray and fast for them. His prayer reflected his heart's passion and also offers a pattern for our prayers.

First, Nehemiah acknowledged who God is: "the great and awesome God." When we focus on who God is, it helps to put our own problems into proper perspective. Next Nehemiah acknowledged who he himself was: God's servant. Then Nehemiah confessed his own sins and the sins of the Israelites.

Awed, humbled and forgiven—Nehemiah reminded God of his promises to his people. He recounted God's promises to the children of Israel and interceded for his people, asking God to hear his prayer and favor him.

What situation has brought you to tears? If it is enough to touch your heart, it's enough to bring you to your knees. Follow Nehemiah's pattern: Acknowledge who God is and who you are, confess your sins and remind God of his promises.

2 Kings 19:14-19

Hezekiah received the letter from the messengers and read it. Then he went up to the temple of the Lord and spread it out before the Lord. And Hezekiah prayed to the Lord : "O Lord, God of Israel, enthroned between the cherubim, you alone are God over all the kingdoms of the earth. You have made heaven and earth. Give ear, O Lord, and hear; open your eyes, O Lord, and see; listen to the words Sennacherib has sent to insult the living God.

"It is true, O Lord, that the Assyrian kings have laid waste these nations and their lands. They have thrown their gods into the fire and destroyed them, for they were not gods but only wood and stone, fashioned by men's hands. Now, O Lord our God, deliver us from his hand, so that all kingdoms on earth may know that you alone, O Lord, are God."

K ing Hezekiah, one of Judah's godly kings, endured taunts and intimidation at the hands of his enemies. When a letter came from the Assyrian King Sennacherib threatening that he would conquer Judah, Hezekiah had his own disaster plan. He laid out the letter before the Lord and prayed. In his faithfulness, God listened and delivered the Israelites.

What do you do when you encounter a terrible scenario that seems to have no solution? When tragedy roars down on you like a tsunami? When something or someone truly terrifying marches your way? Do you curl up in retreat? Do you strike back in retaliation? Or do you lay the situation out before God and trust him to show you what to do?

Wouldn't it be wonderful if down the road everyone who looks at the end of your story has reason to exclaim, "Who is a God like yours!"

"Now fear the L<small>ORD</small> and serve him with all faithfulness. Throw away the gods your forefathers worshiped beyond the River and in Egypt, and serve the L<small>ORD</small>. But if serving the L<small>ORD</small> seems undesirable to you, then choose for yourselves this day whom you will serve, whether the gods your forefathers served beyond the river, or the gods of the Amorites, in whose land you are living. But as for me and my household, we will serve the L<small>ORD</small>."

Then the people answered, "Far be it from us to forsake the L<small>ORD</small> to serve other gods! It was the L<small>ORD</small> our God himself who brought us and our fathers up out of Egypt, from that land of slavery, and performed those great signs before our eyes. He protected us on our entire journey and among all the nations through which we traveled. And the L<small>ORD</small> drove out before us all the nations, including the Amorites, who lived in the land. We too will serve the L<small>ORD</small>, because he is our God."

Choose wisely

Joshua had faithfully led the Israelites into the promised land. Yet the time had come for the new nation to move forward. So he gave his farewell address, urging the people to choose wisely whom they would serve. He challenged them to make a conscious decision not to become entangled with the old gods but to serve the one true God. Knowing that the best leaders lead by example, he told the people that he and his household would "serve the Lord."

It has been said that a choice repeated becomes a habit, a habit develops your character, and your character determines your destiny. Joshua's choices led to a destiny of faithful leadership and a family of faith.

You are faced with the same choices today: to lead your household in serving the Lord or to serve the gods of the world. Will you choose wisely?

On a Sabbath Jesus was teaching in one of the synagogues, and a woman was there who had been crippled by a spirit for eighteen years. She was bent over and could not straighten up at all. When Jesus saw her, he called her forward and said to her, "Woman, you are set free from your infirmity." Then he put his hands on her, and immediately she straightened up and praised God.

Indignant because Jesus had healed on the Sabbath, the synagogue ruler said to the people, "There are six days for work. So come and be healed on those days, not on the Sabbath."

The Lord answered him, "You hypocrites! Doesn't each of you on the Sabbath untie his ox or donkey from the stall and lead it out to give it water? Then should not this woman, a daughter of Abraham, whom Satan has kept bound for eighteen long years, be set free on the Sabbath day from what bound her?"

When he said this, all his opponents were humiliated, but the people were delighted with all the wonderful things he was doing.

The woman in the synagogue had spent eighteen years being overlooked. But when Jesus saw her, he didn't turn away. He didn't pretend not to see her. Instead, he spoke to her and touched her. She was set free from her infirmity. Her eighteen years of living with a crooked body dropped away, and she stood straight and tall, seeing Jesus face-to-face.

In that compassionate interaction, Jesus showed us that, first of all, we need to see others—to look at them and acknowledge their presence as God's creation, precious in his sight. When we look into their eyes, we'll see a human being and not a deformity, disability or limitation. Second, we need to speak to that person as we would anyone. Third, we need to be willing to touch them if it's appropriate. Human touch is a mysterious, powerful tool that communicates worth and significance through something as simple as a handshake, a touch on the shoulder or a hug.

Everyone needs to know that they are valued. When we begin to see others as Jesus does—as human beings with value and significance—we might become the window through which they can see Jesus for themselves.

In the fifth year of Joram son of Ahab king of Israel, when Jehoshaphat was king of Judah, Jehoram son of Jehoshaphat began his reign as king of Judah. He was thirty-two years old when he became king, and he reigned in Jerusalem eight years. He walked in the ways of the kings of Israel, as the house of Ahab had done, for he married a daughter of Ahab. He did evil in the eyes of the LORD. Nevertheless, for the sake of his servant David, the LORD was not willing to destroy Judah. He had promised to maintain a lamp for David and his descendants forever.

God doesn't forget his promises; he remembers them regardless of how much time passes. King Jehoram, Judah's fifth king, reigned for eight years. Unlike his faithful father, Jehoshaphat, who worshipped the Lord, Jehoram "did evil in the eyes of the Lord" and incurred God's anger. God allowed the Philistines, Arabians and Cushites to invade and plunder the land. Jehoram died a painful death and was denied burial in the tomb of the kings (see 2 Chronicles 21:16-20).

Because of Jehoram's evil actions, his reign ended painfully and abruptly. But God allowed Jehoram's grandson to survive. God remembered his promise to King David that he would preserve a godly remnant so that a Savior, his only Son, could be born through the tribe of Judah. Roughly 600 years after the final book in the Old Testament was written, God kept his promises by sending Jesus in his perfect time in his perfect way.

The sad truth is that people do break promises. They fail to keep their word. And this breaks our hearts. But no matter how many promises have been broken, no matter how many people have let us down, God never will. He is faithful, even if his promises take time to come to fruition.

Jeremiah 17:5, 9-10

*This is what the L*ᴏʀᴅ *says:*
"Cursed is the one who trusts in man,
who depends on flesh for his strength
*and whose heart turns away from the L*ᴏʀᴅ*.*

"The heart is deceitful above all things
and beyond cure.
Who can understand it?

*"I the L*ᴏʀᴅ *search the heart*
and examine the mind,
to reward a man according to his conduct,
according to what his deeds deserve."

When you hear the words "heart failure," you panic. Many women have lost parents, friends or a husband to a weakly pumping heart. Maybe you suffer from heart disease. But even if your physical heart is healthy, your spiritual heart is a terminal case. The prophet Jeremiah described it this way: "The heart is... beyond cure."

Maybe you believe your own spiritual heart works just fine. Your own efforts will cure you—or so you think. "Go with your heart," the world says. What do you believe? Do you agree with Jeremiah's assessment or are you feeling that the world is right on this point?

To determine the state of your heart you need the help of a professional. More thoroughly than any doctor's diagnosis, God probes the inner workings of our hearts. Not doing what we need to do to heal our physical heart will allow the damage to progress. Disregard of our spiritual health is just as devastating.

The bad news: You have a broken heart. The good news: God can cure the incurable.

Beware of turning to evil,
*   which you seem to prefer to affliction.*

God is exalted in his power.
*   Who is a teacher like him?*

Who has prescribed his ways for him,
*   or said to him, "You have done wrong?"*

Remember to extol his work,
*   which men have praised in song.*

All mankind has seen it;
*   men gaze on it from afar.*

How great is God—beyond our understanding!
*   The number of his years is past finding out.*

He draws up the drops of water,
*   which distill as rain to the streams;*

the clouds pour down their moisture
*   and abundant showers fall on mankind.*

Who?

While great strides have been made in observing, predicting and understanding the weather, no one has been able to change it. Why? Because while human beings have studied the what, when, and where and how, they often have forgotten to ask the most important question of all. Who?

Job's friend, Elihu, didn't subscribe to the weather channel or own a farmer's almanac. He understood, however, that God controls it all. "He draws up the drops of water, which distill as rain to the streams, the clouds pour down their moisture and abundant showers fall on mankind." He could have said, "I don't understand the process of condensation and precipitation, but I do understand that God is in control."

The first words in the Bible are, "In the beginning God." While we might not understand all the intricate details and secrets of life, we can hold on to this: God set the universe in motion and sustains it.

Are you going through a difficult situation in your life right now? Instead of trying to fix it or control it, rather than trying to figure out the what, when, where and why of your struggle, focus instead on Who.

The Reubenites, the Gadites and the half-tribe of Manasseh had 44,760 men ready for military service—able-bodied men who could handle shield and sword, who could use a bow, and who were trained for battle. They waged war against the Hagrites, Jetur, Naphish and Nodab. They were helped in fighting them, and God handed the Hagrites and all their allies over to them, because they cried out to him during the battle. He answered their prayers, because they trusted in him. They seized the livestock of the Hagrites—fifty thousand camels, two hundred fifty thousand sheep and two thousand donkeys. They also took one hundred thousand people captive, and many others fell slain, because the battle was God's. And they occupied the land until the exile.

Imagine ranks of warriors stretching as far as the eye can see. Nearly 45,000 strapping young men—weapon-savvy, war-hungry and expertly trained—fingering their bows and sword hilts impatiently. They had trained for this battle. As the battle got underway and the screams tore at their eardrums, you could hear something else: the cries of the warriors calling out to God for help. He was the secret weapon in the battle. And they trusted him for the victory.

Let's face it: Life is more a battlefield than a playground. We fight battles within ourselves—against insecurity, anxiety, depression. We fight for spiritual territory rather than for plots of land. We fight against the fallen things in this world: materialism, greed, selfishness, addiction, violence, apathy, prejudice, injustice.

As soldiers in God's army we are called to do battle with evil by putting on the armor of God. Take up your shield of faith, the helmet of salvation and the sword of the Spirit. Don't hesitate to utilize your secret weapon by praying to the Lord of Hosts, and trust him to hear your prayers. He's the one who will lead you to win your battle because he has already won the war.

Amos 8:4-10

Hear this, you who trample
*   the needy*
and do away with the poor of the
*   land, saying,*
"When will the New Moon be over
*   that we may sell grain,*
*   and the Sabbath be ended*
*   that we may market wheat?"—*
*   skimping the measure,*
*   boosting the price*
*   and cheating with dishonest scales,*

buying the poor with silver
*   and the needy for a pair of sandals,*
*   selling even the sweepings with*
*   the wheat.*

The Lord has sworn by the Pride
*   of Jacob: "I will never forget*
*   anything they have done.*

"Will not the land tremble for this,

and all who live in it mourn?
*   The whole land will rise like the Nile;*
*   it will be stirred up and then sink*
*   like the river of Egypt.*

"In that day," declares the
*   Sovereign Lord,*
"I will make the sun go down
*   at noon*
*   and darken the earth in*
*   broad daylight.*

"I will turn your religious feasts
*   into mourning*
*   and all your singing into weeping.*
*   I will make all of you*
*   wear sackcloth*
*   and shave your heads.*
*   I will make that time like mourning*
*   for an only son*
*   and the end of it like a bitter day."*

What about the poor?

Ask your neighbor or coworker to list the "top ten" sins and you will probably hear a version of the Ten Commandments. Murder, stealing, lying and adultery would probably head the list. But when God revealed to Amos that he was about to bring judgment upon his people, he cited Israel's treatment of the poor as cause for punishment. In startling imagery, God said Israel had "trampled" the needy and cheated the poor. The poor, the victims of Israel's greed and exploitation, had no recourse but to appeal to God. And God listened.

How does the way you live reveal your concern for the poor? Are the poor an afterthought? A nuisance? Amos's message challenges us to serve the poverty-stricken in ways besides simply giving money. Volunteering in a food pantry or rescue mission, for example. But are there ways to take our compassion one step further? How can we speak up to make sure the poor aren't exploited? How can we vote for policies and practices that are equitable?

It is God's desire that we be willing to share what we have with those in need and help the poor whenever we can. When we do, our hearts beat in time with his.

I wanted to see what was worthwhile for men to do under heaven during the few days of their lives.

I undertook great projects: I built houses for myself and planted vineyards. I made gardens and parks and planted all kinds of fruit trees in them. I made reservoirs to water groves of flourishing trees. I bought male and female slaves and had other slaves who were born in my house. I also owned more herds and flocks than anyone in Jerusalem before me. I amassed silver and gold for myself, and the treasure of kings and provinces. I acquired men and women singers, and a harem as well—the delights of the heart of man. I became greater by far than anyone in Jerusalem before me. In all this my wisdom stayed with me.

I denied myself nothing my
eyes desired;
I refused my heart no pleasure.
My heart took delight in all
my work,
and this was the reward for all
my labor.

Yet when I surveyed all that my
hands had done
and what I had toiled to
achieve,
everything was meaningless,
a chasing after the wind;
nothing was gained
under the sun.

ave you ever tried to catch the wind? Perhaps you once launched a kite on a passing breeze or trimmed your sails to harness the swirling air currents to propel your sailboat forward. But did you honestly catch the wind—or did it catch you? Wind is elusive. It is intangible.

Solomon discovered that finding pleasure is as elusive as catching the wind. He pursued everything imaginable to achieve lasting bliss. But the smartest man alive still had a restless mind. The richest man in the world couldn't buy happiness. The most powerful person in the kingdom was unable to satisfy his own heart.

Securing happiness on our own is like trying to catch the wind. Try to chase it, but it will always remain just out of reach. The Bible teaches us that instead of searching for happiness, we should allow God's joy and peace to reign in our hearts. Instead of striving for the things we think will satisfy, we can learn to find true contentment by looking to God, whatever our circumstance. The true source of pleasure is God. Don't waste your time trying to catch the wind. Instead, find true happiness by laying hold of the Wind Maker.

God said, "As for me, this is my covenant with you: You will be the father of many nations. No longer will you be called Abram; your name will be Abraham, for I have made you a father of many nations. I will make you very fruitful; I will make nations of you, and kings will come from you. I will establish my covenant as an everlasting covenant between me and you and your descendants after you for the generations to come, to be your God and the God of your descendants after you. The whole land of Canaan, where you are now an alien, I will give as an everlasting possession to you and your descendants after you; and I will be their God."

God also said to Abraham, "As for Sarai your wife, you are no longer to call her Sarai; her name will be Sarah. I will bless her and will surely give you a son by her. I will bless her so that she will be the mother of nations; kings of peoples will come from her."

For Sarah's husband, a baby brought the prospect of being the father of a nation, of seeing his name carried throughout generations. For Abraham, the baby meant his lineage was now secure. He smiled in satisfaction as he contemplated the future. But not Sarah. The idea of mothering an entire race of people was beyond her for the moment. She was content to just let herself be entirely dazzled by the innocence in her baby's eyes, the scent of his flawless skin, the softness of his tiny hands.

Maybe Sarah had a motherly tendency to focus on the now, and Abraham envisioned several generations into the future, but God had eternity clearly in view. It wasn't about the promise as much as it was about the Promise Maker.

Behind the promise, Sarah could see the unseen Promise Maker. Far beyond the tiniest branch of the family tree that Abraham could envision, eternity stretched outward. The indescribable delight and pleasure of holding her son was meant to teach Sarah about the rapture of God cradling her in the palm of his hand.

2 Kings 22:1-2

Josiah was eight years old when he became king, and he reigned in Jerusalem thirty-one years. His mother's name was Jedidah daughter of Adaiah; she was from Bozkath. He did what was right in the eyes of the LORD and walked in all the ways of his father David, not turning aside to the right or to the left.

Life condensed

Condensed soup. Condensed milk. Condensed books. We like all sorts of things that are condensed, consolidated, compressed, abridged or abbreviated. The condensed version of King Josiah's life is found in a single sentence. Thirty-one words in one verse sum up the essence of his entire life: "He did what was right in the eyes of the LORD and walked in all the ways of his father David, not turning aside to the right or to the left." Amazing! Concise! Josiah walked the path of righteousness without swerving.

If your life were condensed into a short synopsis—one brief sentence—what would be said of you? As we care for families and do our work, it's easy to become sidetracked from our primary purpose: pleasing God. It is easier to give lip service to spiritual things than to stay on course, keeping in step with the Spirit.

Eventually, someone will write your obituary or eulogy. Your life will be abridged into a few brief sentences and paragraphs. What will be said of you? More important, how will God summarize your life? Let it be said of you that you did what was right in the eyes of the Lord.

One day Naomi her mother-in-law said to her, "My daughter, should I not try to find a home for you, where you will be well provided for? Is not Boaz, with whose servant girls you have been, a kinsman of ours? Tonight he will be winnowing barley on the threshing floor. Wash and perfume yourself, and put on your best clothes. Then go down to the threshing floor, but don't let him know you are there until he has finished eating and drinking. When he lies down, note the place where he is lying. Then go and uncover his feet and lie down. He will tell you what to do."

"I will do whatever you say," Ruth answered. So she went down to the threshing floor and did everything her mother-in-law told her to do. …

When Ruth came to her mother-in-law, Naomi asked, "How did it go, my daughter?"

She told her everything Boaz had done for her and added, "He gave me these six measures of barley, saying, 'Don't go back to your mother-in-law empty-handed.' "

Naomi said, "Wait, my daughter, until you find out what happens. For the man will not rest until the matter is settled today."

Learning to wait

"How did it go, my daughter?" Naomi asked her daughter-in-law Ruth. Ruth had just returned from spending an evening with Boaz. Like a schoolgirl describing her first experience falling in love, the words tumbled out of her. The way her daughter-in-law smiled and mindlessly fingered a lock of her hair whenever she said Boaz' name reminded Naomi of an earlier time: a time when the very thought of her former husband, Elimelech, "Eli" as she liked to call him, sent a chill of excitement through her.

But that was before their hometown of Bethlehem became a poorhouse, before the famine, before the move to Moab, before immeasurable heartache and loss. When she lost her husband and then both sons, she was sure life would never be the same. And it never was.

Naomi had scoffed at the irony. Her mother had named her "Pleasant." What was pleasant about her life now? However, from the ruddy soil of her sorrow, seeds of hope sprouted from one small word: wait. So Naomi offered Ruth the best advice she could. "Wait, wait, my daughter, until you find out what happens." Just wait.

Job's wife said to him, "Are you still holding on to your integrity? Curse God and die!"

He replied, "You are talking like a foolish woman. Shall we accept good from God, and not trouble?" In all this, Job did not sin in what he said.

When Job's three friends, Eliphaz the Temanite, Bildad the Shuhite and Zophar the Naamathite, heard about all the troubles that had come upon him, they set out from their homes and met together by agreement to go and sympathize with him and comfort him. When they saw him from a distance, they could hardly recognize him; they began to weep aloud, and they tore their robes and sprinkled dust on their heads. Then they sat on the ground with him for seven days and seven nights. No one said a word to him, because they saw how great his suffering was.

J ob was suffering. All of his children, servants, flocks and herds were gone. His health and well-being were decimated. Job's wife bitterly responded, "Curse God and die!" As much as she, too, must have been suffering, Job's wife talked too much and too soon. Job's friends tried to explain away his misfortunes and strongly blamed Job. But at the beginning, they got it right by recognizing that nothing they could say could assuage his grief. Here, they offered him not words but the comfort of their presence.

When we encounter friends who have suffered great loss, it is easy to drop off a casserole, send a sympathy card or say, "Call me if you need anything." We often rely on pat answers. "God knows best; all things work together for good." Sometimes we speak too much or too soon.

But perhaps Job's friends stumbled onto one key to mourning with those who mourn: Have the wisdom to know when to talk and when to stay silent. The next time you find yourself eye-to-eye with someone in grief, don't worry about what you will say. God will give you the words to speak and the wisdom to know when to keep silent.

We continually remember before our God and Father your work produced by faith, your labor prompted by love, and your endurance inspired by hope in our Lord Jesus Christ.

For we know, brothers loved by God, that he has chosen you, because our gospel came to you not simply with words, but also with power, with the Holy Spirit and with deep conviction. You know how we lived among you for your sake. You became imitators of us and of the Lord; in spite of severe suffering, you welcomed the message with the joy given by the Holy Spirit. And so you became a model to all the believers in Macedonia and Achaia. The Lord's message rang out from you not only in Macedonia and Achaia—your faith in God has become known everywhere. Therefore we do not need to say anything about it, for they themselves report what kind of reception you gave us. They tell how you turned to God from idols to serve the living and true God, and to wait for his Son from heaven, whom he raised from the dead—Jesus, who rescues us from the coming wrath.

One of the most illuminating names of God is the one especially revealed by our Lord Jesus Christ, the name of the Father. While God had been called throughout the ages by many other names, expressing other aspects of His character, Christ alone has revealed him to us under the all-inclusive name of Father—a name that holds within itself all other names of wisdom and power, and above all a name of love and goodness, a name that embodies for us a perfect supply for all our needs.

But God is not only a father, He is a mother as well, and we have all known mothers whose love and tenderness have been without bound or limit. And it is very certain that the God who created them both, and who is himself father and mother in one, could never have created earthly fathers and mothers who were more tender and more loving than he is himself. Therefore if we want to know what sort of a Father He is, we must heap together all the best of all the fathers and mothers we have ever known or can imagine, and we must tell ourselves that this is only a faint image of God, our father in heaven.

Psalm 1:1-6

Blessed is the man
who does not walk in the counsel of the wicked
or stand in the way of sinners
or sit in the seat of mockers.

But his delight is in the law of the LORD,
and on his law he meditates day and night.

He is like a tree planted by streams of water,
which yields its fruit in season
and whose leaf does not wither.
Whatever he does prospers.

Not so the wicked!
They are like chaff
that the wind blows away.

Therefore the wicked will not stand in the judgment,
nor sinners in the assembly of the righteous.

For the LORD watches over the way of the righteous,
but the way of the wicked will perish.

W hat gives you delight? You know, that sense of unparalleled joy, that amazing degree of enjoyment and pleasure even to the point of rapture. That's how the dictionary defines delight. But how do you define delight?

The psalmist defines delight as immersing oneself in the law of the Lord. He sings of the person who finds joy in listening to God's voice in Scripture, who discovers with pleasure, "the riches of the wisdom and knowledge of God" (Romans 11:33). For this person, meditating on the Scriptures is not a duty that fulfills a certain obligation, but it is willingly devoting spare time, staying up late into the night immersed in the Bible.

And what is the result of this constant delight in God's Word? One becomes like a tree planted by a river. You've seen them—tall, vital trees, well-watered because they are rooted deep in the stream. This tree is resplendent with foliage in rich shades of green. It's a tree that can withstand biting frost, harsh winds and blazing sun. A person who delights in God's Word will prosper and have integrity, and will speak truthfully and exhibit stability and strength. This is the person who will reflect the face of God like a river reflects the sun in dappled waves. This one is truly blessed.

Psalm 42:1-3, 5-6

As the deer pants for streams of water,
so my soul pants for you, O God.

My soul thirsts for God, for the living God.
When can I go and meet with God?

My tears have been my food
day and night,
while men say to me all day long,
"Where is your God?"

Why are you downcast, O my soul?
Why so disturbed within me?
Put your hope in God,
for I will yet praise him,
my Savior and my God.

My soul is downcast within me;
therefore I will remember you
from the land of the Jordan,
the heights of Hermon—from Mount Mizar.

Exiled north to Jordan and overflowing with a longing to return to Jerusalem, the psalmist voiced his deep sadness. Rather than denying or minimizing his pain, he clearly identified his sorrow and proclaimed his thirst for God. Then what? The psalmist spoke to his soul! Was he mad? Did he have a personality disorder? No! He practiced the secret to overcoming hopelessness—the hopelessness that can trickle into our hearts and minds until we find ourselves in the rushing current tumbling toward a waterfall of despair.

The psalmist encouraged his soul to praise God—in other words, to acknowledge, affirm and adore God's character, even when he was feeling downcast in spirit or disturbed in heart. Our souls need similar encouragement. When we choose to dwell upon God's character, we always have something to praise him about: his loving kindness. Goodness, power, faithfulness and mercy. When we choose to live close to God's heart we overflow with delight and joy.

If you are submerged in pain, sorrow, despair or confusion, maybe you need to give your soul a good talking to. What will you say?

Psalm 92:1-8

It is good to praise the Lᴏʀᴅ
*   and make music to your name, O Most High,*

to proclaim your love in the morning
*   and your faithfulness at night,*

to the music of the ten-stringed lyre
*   and the melody of the harp.*

For you make me glad by your deeds, O Lᴏʀᴅ;
*   I sing for joy at the works of your hands.*

How great are your works, O Lᴏʀᴅ,
*   how profound your thoughts!*

The senseless man does not know,
*   fools do not understand,*

that though the wicked spring up like grass
*   and all evildoers flourish,*
*   they will be forever destroyed.*

But you, O Lᴏʀᴅ, are exalted forever.

God, who gave the crow his harsh caw and dark plumage, also granted the cardinal his lovely song and a coat that can be seen half a block away. The God who created broccoli also surprises us with the taste of watermelon in the season we need it most.

The Creator sprinkled the world with butterflies and fireflies and gave us noisy, refreshing creeks and waterfalls. He hid treasures of gold and copper, diamonds and rubies inside his mountains. And he gave us voices and even rounded up psalmists to write some of the words we can sing.

In Psalm 92 the psalmist recites several reasons why "it is good to praise the LORD." This God deserves the praises of all his creatures: people, birds—and even the stones of the field. Whether our instrument is a flute, a guitar or our own off-key singing voices, God wants our praise. Declaring his love and faithfulness morning, noon and night is good. The ability to praise our Maker in song and words is a gift that only humans have. Use that gift and lift up a chorus of praise today.

Simeon took him in his arms and praised God, saying:
"Sovereign Lord, as you
have promised,
you now dismiss your servant
in peace.
For my eyes have seen
your salvation,
which you have prepared in
the sight of all people,
a light for revelation to the Gentiles
and for glory to your
people Israel."

The child's father and mother marveled at what was said about him. Then Simeon blessed them and said to Mary, his mother: "This child is destined to cause the falling and rising of many in Israel, and to be a sign that will be spoken against, so that the thoughts of many hearts will be revealed. And a sword will pierce your own soul too."

There was also a prophetess, Anna, the daughter of Phanuel, of the tribe of Asher. She was very old; she had lived with her husband seven years after her marriage, and then was a widow until she was eighty-four. She never left the temple but worshiped night and day, fasting and praying. Coming up to them at that very moment, she gave thanks to God and spoke about the child to all who were looking forward to the redemption of Jerusalem.

Anna was old. Married for only seven years, a widow until age eighty-four, Anna had witnessed the passing of decade after decade. Her world was not a large one, as she was consigned to living in the temple and devoted herself to fasting and prayer; she mostly worshiped and waited. The years of waiting were finally over when she spotted him: the precious infant lying in the young mother's arms. Angels had announced this child's birth. Now an aged woman became another in the line of those who sang the chorus of annunciation.

We live in a youth-oriented culture. Older women can easily feel marginalized—as if their days of usefulness are past. Yet Scripture reminds us that God reserves some of his most significant assignments to women who have attained the maturity to handle them— like Anna the prophetess.

Angels and an elderly woman announced the birth of the Savior of the world. Approximately thirty-three years later, angels and a select group of women proclaimed the astounding news of his resurrection from the dead. Age and gender present no barrier when God entrusts us with a divine message or mission.

Then the man brought me to the gate facing east, and I saw the glory of the God of Israel coming from the east. His voice was like the roar of rushing waters, and the land was radiant with his glory. The vision I saw was like the vision I had seen when he came to destroy the city and like the visions I had seen by the Kebar River, and I fell facedown. The glory of the LORD entered the temple through the gate facing east. Then the Spirit lifted me up and brought me into the inner court, and the glory of the LORD filled the temple.

God in you

Picture a consuming fire, a cumulus cloud, a rainbow on an overcast day. In the Old Testament, God gives us many compelling images of his glory. At that time, his glory dwelled in temples made by human hands. And one day, as Ezekiel's grandiose vision details, his glory will fill the temple once again.

The unifying theme of God's glory, in both the Old and New Testaments, is holiness. While we wait for God's glory to fill the temple one day, the God of the universe makes his home in human hearts. When Jesus returned to heaven, he left the Holy Spirit to fill the hearts of his people. God resides within those who have invited him. Our bodies are temples of the Lord, says the apostle Paul in 1 Corinthians 6:19, so we must honor them by pursuing and practicing holiness.

Ezekiel's vision should challenge us to make a choice. We can fill our temple with sin or with God's glory. Ezekiel's vision ultimately speaks of a time when the temple will no longer be defiled by sin. Instead, God's glory, his beauty, splendor and majesty will fill the temple.

2 Corinthians 2:5-11

If anyone has caused grief, he has not so much grieved me as he has grieved all of you, to some extent— not to put it too severely. The punishment inflicted on him by the majority is sufficient for him. Now instead, you ought to forgive and comfort him, so that he will not be overwhelmed by excessive sorrow. I urge you, therefore, to reaffirm your love for him. The reason I wrote you was to see if you would stand the test and be obedient in everything. If you forgive anyone, I also forgive him. And what I have forgiven—if there was anything to forgive—I have forgiven in the sight of Christ for your sake, in order that Satan might not outwit us. For we are not unaware of his schemes.

Restoring an errant spouse

In 1 Corinthians 5:1-5 Paul told the church in Corinth to deal with a sticky problem. A member of the church was having an affair with "his father's wife," which was an offense even to the jaded unbelievers in pagan Corinth. Paul said the man should be put out of the church until he repented.

It's possible that the man discussed in 1 Corinthians 5:1-5 was the person Paul was referring to in 2 Corinthians 2:5-11. If so, the apostle had learned that the man had repented of his sin, and Paul was therefore guiding the church through the challenge of restoring the man to fellowship. Paul's advice is useful for us today as we deal with Christians who have repented of sin.

Restoration is difficult. The sins of believers profoundly affect us. We are angry as we struggle with the pain of violated trust. And the situation is especially difficult when it is our spouse who has deeply hurt us.

The first step toward restoration begins when we reaffirm our love for the offender by extending forgiveness and comfort. Praying for God's grace in our weakness so that we may be merciful, just as our heavenly Father is merciful, will help us take that step.

Therefore, although in Christ I could be bold and order you to do what you ought to do, yet I appeal to you on the basis of love. I then, as Paul—an old man and now also a prisoner of Christ Jesus—I appeal to you for my son Onesimus, who became my son while I was in chains. Formerly he was useless to you, but now he has become useful both to you and to me.

I am sending him—who is my very heart—back to you. I would have liked to keep him with me so that he could take your place in helping me while I am in chains for the gospel. But I did not want to do anything without your consent, so that any favor you do will be spontaneous and not forced. Perhaps the reason he was separated from you for a little while was that you might have him back for good—no longer as a slave, but better than a slave, as a dear brother. He is very dear to me but even dearer to you, both as a man and as a brother in the Lord.

Philemon's slave Onesimus had run away, met Paul in Rome and become a Christian. Now Paul was sending the slave back to his master, urging Philemon to receive Onesimus, not as mere property, but as a brother. Instead of butting heads with Philemon, Paul extended a hand of love. Was this a sign of weakness? Psychological manipulation?

Both possibilities and a variety of others enter a marital relationship. Sometimes we badger one another. Sometimes, like goats poised for battle on a mountain trail, we come close to butting heads. Too often we allow our emotions to derail relationships because we are blinded by excessive self-importance. The strength of our emotions, especially when we are at odds with each other, inflates our tendency for self-preservation and diminishes our sense of the other's importance in our lives. We need to keep relationships personal and issues impersonal as we build faithfulness with one another.

Disagreements are inevitable in any relationship. But the ways in which we work through them can bind us more tightly together in love. Paul's kindness to Philemon offers a very good example to follow.

This is what the Sovereign LORD says: "In the first month on the first day you are to take a young bull without defect and purify the sanctuary. The priest is to take some of the blood of the sin offering and put it on the doorposts of the temple, on the four corners of the upper ledge of the altar and on the gateposts of the inner court. You are to do the same on the seventh day of the month for anyone who sins unintentionally or through ignorance; so you are to make atonement for the temple.

"In the first month on the fourteenth day you are to observe the Passover, a feast lasting seven days, during which you shall eat bread made without yeast. On that day the prince is to provide a bull as a sin offering for himself and for all the people of the land. Every day during the seven days of the Feast he is to provide seven bulls and seven rams without defect as a burnt offering to the LORD, and a male goat for a sin offering."

Once and for all

re you nagged by guilty feelings over your sins? Do you replay mistakes in your head over and over? For the Israelites, sins must have been almost continually on their minds. Just when they finished one sacrifice, it was time for another. Because they could not permanently remove the sin of the people, the blood of countless animals spilled down the altar year after year.

Only one sacrifice has ever been sufficient to atone for people's sin once for all time. Through Jesus Christ's death on the cross, we can receive forgiveness from sin—permanently. There is no additional sacrifice needed.

Satan would like nothing more than to make us feel that we are not forgiven. Satan reminds us of our sins, holding them over our heads. But when we believe his lies, we deny the truth of what Christ accomplished. The next time you feel guilt start to surface, recall the permanent and perfect sacrifice of Christ. He paid for your sin. All of it.

As Jesus and his disciples were on their way, he came to a village where a woman named Martha opened her home to him. She had a sister called Mary, who sat at the the Lord's feet listening to what he said. But Martha was distracted by all the preparations that had to be made. She came to him and asked, "Lord, don't you care that my sister has left me to do the work by myself? Tell her to help me!"

"Martha, Martha," the Lord answered, "you are worried and upset about many things, but only one thing is needed. Mary has chosen what is better, and it will not be taken away from her."

Too busy

We face the same choice that confronted Martha. We can dismiss the implications of Jesus' words for us, especially when our time is limited and we are juggling so many other demands. Or we can face our need and begin working to know God better. The real choice is not whether we will become thinkers or doers. We are called to be both. But we will be better at both if we heed Christ's call to dig deeply into the heart of God.

Mary and Martha learned the hard way, and we do too. If our own struggles have taught us anything, it is that our greatest need is to know God better and that we are not alone. To be blunt, life is simply too demanding and overwhelming at times to think we can manage without knowing the one who rules the winds and waves that batter our little vessel.

There is much to do and more to learn. Not even a lifetime will be enough to know God completely. But our smallest efforts will be richly rewarded, for the time it takes to dig deep into the heart of God is often repaid by striking a vein of gold or an oil gusher. The effort is repaid with joy and power beyond all expectation.

Hosea 11:1-4, 8

God said, "When Israel was a child, I loved him,
and out of Egypt I called my son.

"But the more I called Israel,
the further they went from me.
They sacrificed to the Baals
and they burned incense to images.

"It was I who taught Ephraim to walk,
taking them by the arms;
but they did not realize
it was I who healed them.

"I led them with cords of human kindness,
with ties of love;
I lifted the yoke from their neck
and bent down to feed them.

"How can I give you up, Ephraim?
How can I hand you over, Israel? ...
My heart is changed within me;
all my compassion is aroused.

osea describes a God who leads his people and loves them like the perfect Father he is, a father who has every reason to be angry with his children when they run in the opposite direction, discounting the gifts he has given them, honoring everything and anything but him, and refusing to listen or to come home to him. Even so, God's "compassion is aroused," writes the prophet Hosea. Though the people deserve it, he "will not come in wrath." Instead, he comes to them in love.

Hosea reminds his people that it is time to stop running away and start running back into God's open arms. God will not give up. No matter how many miles from home you feel, no matter how long it's been since you whispered a prayer or listened for God's voice, the journey back to where you belong is one step away.

All the people left from the Hittites, Amorites, Perizzites, Hivites and Jebusites (these peoples were not Israelites), that is, their descendants remaining in the land, whom the Israelites had not destroyed—these Solomon conscripted for his slave labor force, as it is to this day. But Solomon did not make slaves of the Israelites for his work; they were his fighting men, commanders of his captains, and commanders of his chariots and charioteers. They were also King Solomon's chief officials—two hundred and fifty officials supervising the men.

Solomon brought Pharaoh's daughter up from the City of David to the palace he had built for her, for he said, "My wife must not live in the palace of David king of Israel, because the places the ark of the LORD has entered are holy."

2 Chronicles 8 tells us that Solomon married an Egyptian princess. Pharoah's daughter was an ironic choice for the wisest man on earth. Was his memory too short that he did not recall the Israelites' miraculous escape from bondage to his wife's ancestors? And even if his wife was a believer in the true God, surely she had servants who worshiped Egyptian gods. Solomon recognized that God's holiness must take precedence over his wife's comfort, so he moved her and her household to the outskirts of Jerusalem. He separated her from God's holy place.

God knows the agony of loving those who, at present, want nothing to do with him. Think of all the people he created who openly reject him. Yet he still loves them and shows by example that his "kindness ... leads them toward repentance" (Romans 2:4).

In your own circumstances, follow God's example by being kind but firm. Be faithful to keep yourself wholly holy. By doing this you can help win your spouse, parent, child, colleague or friend to true belief.

Now a man of the house of Levi married a Levite woman, and she became pregnant and gave birth to a son. When she saw that he was a fine child, she hid him for three months. But when she could hide him no longer, she got a papyrus basket for him and coated it with tar and pitch. Then she placed the child in it and put it among the reeds along the bank of the Nile. His sister stood at a distance to see what would happen to him.

Then Pharaoh's daughter went down to the Nile to bathe, and her attendants were walking along the river bank. She saw the basket among the reeds and sent her slave girl to get it. She opened it and saw the baby. He was crying, and she felt sorry for him. "This is one of the Hebrew babies," she said.

Then his sister asked Pharaoh's daughter, "Shall I go and get one of the Hebrew women to nurse the baby for you?"

"Yes, go," she answered. And the girl went and got the baby's mother.

Before Moses was born, the pharaoh of Egypt issued a cruel edict. To keep the Hebrew people from becoming too powerful, every Hebrew baby boy must be killed. But the Hebrew women waited for the right opportunities to frustrate Pharoah's genocidal plan. The midwives, mother, and sisters subverted the edict and saved some of the babies.

Moses' mother put the baby Moses in a basket and placed it in the Nile. Moses' sister watched from the shore. Pharoah's daughter joined in the cause by taking the baby Moses out of the reeds and into her heart. Even as Moses was saved from the fate of so many other children, Miriam "stood at a distance to see what would happen to him."

Every newborn baby enters the context of a human story, even though some of those stories are less than hopeful. You may see this and realize how unfair the world is. You want to do something to help but feel sidelined. You wait. You watch. You pray. You want to perform some act of practical compassion. The truth is, sometimes the best action is the sideline action: Wait, watch and pray. God will guide you to action when the time is right.

Isaiah 26:9, 19

My soul yearns for you in the night;
in the morning my spirit longs for you. …

But your dead will live;
their bodies will rise.
You who dwell in the dust,
wake up and shout for joy.
Your dew is like the dew of the morning;
the earth will give birth to her dead.

Markie, who was five years old, seemed unusually fixated on heaven because so many people he loved were already there. "Why would anyone rather stay on earth when heaven is such a great place?" he often asked. "Grammy, I want to go to heaven today!" said Markie. She sighed before responding, "Mark, only Jesus can decide when it's time for us to go to heaven."

Markie is not the first person to feel the tension of longing for heaven while still living here on earth. The prophet Isaiah spoke for generations of believers who have God's promise that this life is not all there is. There is life after death, and one day we'll wake up in heaven. Our time here is only a tiny dash in the line that stretches toward eternity.

We have the rest of our lives to look forward to, and yet we must focus on the rest of today first. We're headed for home, but we're still on the journey.

Hosea 1:2; 3:1-5

When the LORD began to speak through Hosea, the LORD said to him, "Go, take to yourself an adulterous wife and children of unfaithfulness, because the land is guilty of the vilest adultery in departing from the LORD."

The LORD said to me, "Go, show your love to your wife again, though she is loved by another and is an adulteress. Love her as the LORD loves the Israelites, though they turn to other gods and love the sacred raisin cakes."

So I bought her for fifteen shekels of silver and about a homer and a lethek of barley. Then I told her, "You are to live with me many days; you must not be a prostitute or be intimate with any man, and I will live with you."

For the Israelites will live many days without king or prince, without sacrifice or sacred stones, without ephod or idol. Afterward the Israelites will return and seek the LORD their God and David their king. They will come trembling to the LORD and to his blessings in the last days.

The chatter in the marketplace among the women rose to a crescendo as they daily observed the strange and wonderful relationship between Gomer and her husband. She was strange, and he was wonderful—too wonderful for her. It seemed no matter how deeply she wounded her husband, he would not give up on her. She habitually ran from the security of his love to find solace in the arms of strangers. She preferred the emotionless physicality of those she met on the street to his unfailing, undying love. Instead of loving the one who called her by name, she preferred the anonymity of someone with no name, no home and no family.

Gomer herself must have wondered sometimes about the contradictions. Did she ever stop to ask why Hosea so relentlessly and tenderly loved her? Or why she rejected his love? Did she ever doubt her own emotional stability since she proved incapable of commitment? Gomer was crazy to think that her loveless pursuits could satisfy the core needs for fulfillment and security that every woman has. However, it didn't keep her from running away from the very thing she desperately wanted to find—unfailing love. God's love.

1 Timothy 2:1-8

I urge, then, first of all, that requests, prayers, intercession and thanksgiving be made for everyone—for kings and all those in authority, that we may live peaceful and quiet lives in all godliness and holiness. This is good, and pleases God our Savior, who wants all men to be saved and to come to a knowledge of the truth. For there is one God and one mediator between God and men, the man Christ Jesus, who gave himself as a ransom for all men—the testimony given in its proper time. And for this purpose I was appointed a herald and an apostle—I am telling the truth, I am not lying—and a teacher of the true faith to the Gentiles.

I want men everywhere to lift up holy hands in prayer, without anger or disputing.

aul's letter to Timothy encourages us to pray for everyone. How easy it is to become complacent and believe that the prayers of one person don't really matter. But wouldn't it be better to spend our time praying, rather than giving up in frustration, second-guessing or criticizing others?

Just imagine what would happen if each of us took on the serious business of praying for those around us. Not just saying we'll pray, but really praying—asking for God's wisdom, guidance and protection, and giving thanks for people's willingness to serve. Think of what God might do when you commit to pray for the people you know.

Joshua was dressed in filthy clothes as he stood before the angel. The angel said to those who were standing before him, "Take off his filthy clothes."

Then he said to Joshua, "See, I have taken away your sin, and I will put rich garments on you."

Then I said, "Put a clean turban on his head." So they put a clean turban on his head and clothed him, while the angel of the LORD stood by.

The angel of the LORD gave this charge to Joshua: "This is what the LORD Almighty says: 'If you will walk in my ways and keep my requirements, then you will govern my house and have charge of my courts, and I will give you a place among these standing here.

" 'Listen, O high priest Joshua and your associates seated before you, who are men symbolic of things to come: I am going to bring my servant, the Branch. See, the stone I have set in front of Joshua! There are seven eyes on that one stone, and I will engrave an inscription on it,' says the LORD Almighty, 'and I will remove the sin of this land in a single day.' "

Zechariah reveals God's desire to remove Joshua's garments of sin and shame and to replace them—permanently. The new robes are perfectly pure, symbolizing cleansing and forgiveness. How strange it would be if Joshua refused the gift, only to cling to his filthy clothes. In this sense, rejecting God's forgiveness makes as much sense as a woman turning down a free shopping spree. And yet it happens every day. Rather than accepting God's gift of forgiveness, many individuals choose the familiarity of guilt and the comfort of self-condemnation.

God offers forgiveness to us free of charge. It's free because Jesus already paid the bill on the cross; Jesus' resurrection gives incalculable value to the robes of forgiveness. If he had not defeated death, the new clothes he offers would only be temporary. Because he lives, they will never fade or wear out.

Don't settle for grungy, old rags. Hand your "wardrobe" over, so God can give you a whole new look.

Elimelech, Naomi's husband, died, and she was left with her two sons. They married Moabite women, one named Orpah and the other Ruth. After they had lived there about ten years, both Mahlon and Kilion also died, and Naomi was left without her two sons and her husband.

Then Naomi said to her two daughters-in-law, "Go back, each of you, to your mother's home." But Ruth replied, "Don't urge me to leave you or to turn back from you. Where you go I will go, and where you stay I will stay. Your people will be my people and your God my God. Where you die I will die, and there I will be buried."

So Naomi returned from Moab accompanied by Ruth the Moabitess, her daughter-in-law, arriving in Bethlehem as the barley harvest was beginning.

Ruth faced a big decision when her husband died. Although her sister-in-law, Orpah, chose to stay among her people and pagan gods in Moab, Ruth chose to follow her mother-in-law to the land of Judah. There she found new hope, a new husband and a place in the genealogy of the Messiah.

Not all of us have experienced the death of a spouse as Ruth did, but we have all experienced death in some form. Some of us have lost someone dear, leaving emptiness in our hearts. We go on, but we ache for their presence. What do you do in the face of death? Do you blame God, as Naomi did? Do you stay put in nowhere land, as Orpah stayed in Moab? Or do you let God weave your grief into a new story, as Ruth did?

Our faith promises new life. God knows the "deaths" you've experienced. His plans for you are good, though they may look different than you expected. Rest in the knowledge that God uses every circumstance to strengthen your faith in him.

Psalm 86:9-12, 16-17

All the nations you have made
will come and worship before you, O Lord;
they will bring glory to your name.

For you are great and do marvelous deeds;
you alone are God.

Teach me your way, O LORD,
and I will walk in your truth;
give me an undivided heart,
that I may fear your name.

I will praise you, O Lord my God, with all my heart;
I will glorify your name forever.

Turn to me and have mercy on me;
grant your strength to your servant
and save the son of your maidservant.

Give me a sign of your goodness,
that my enemies may see it and be put to shame,
for you, O LORD, have helped me and comforted me.

W hen you approach God in prayer, what are the "givens" you believe about him? That he hears you, forgives you and loves you with a steadfast love? That's how the psalmist describes God. But do you sometimes secretly picture him as an unmerciful judge, wondering if he really will forgive this sin—the one you find yourself repeatedly battling?

Sometimes without realizing it, we project upon God images of our own making—a demanding taskmaster for whom we never can do enough, an exacting parent we can never quite please, a short-tempered boss we easily anger. Yet, this is not the God of the Bible, the God of David, and this is not the real God.

Listen to David's description of the God he knew so intimately. God is not an unmerciful, cruel master but a "forgiving and good" heavenly Father. He is not skimpy with his love, and he does not play favorites. He is not a God who gives love conditionally. Who is this God we serve? This is no impotent God: "You are great and do marvelous deeds."

When you find yourself hesitant to come before God or to wholly trust him, consider what image of God you're holding onto. Is it the real God of Scripture or an imposter? Worship the real God, in spirit and in truth.

Job 1:20-22

At this, Job got up and tore his robe and shaved his head.
Then he fell to the ground in worship and said:

> *"Naked I came from my mother's womb,*
> *and naked I will depart.*
> *The Lord gave and the*
> *Lord has taken away;*
> *may the name of the Lord be praised."*

In all this, Job did not sin by charging God with wrongdoing.

Devastating messages assaulted Job again and again—each one coming while the messenger "was still speaking." Who can even begin to comprehend his sheer horror at learning that all ten of his children were dead? What did Job do? What was his initial response upon hearing of the loss of all he owned and of all he held dear? First he grieved. Job's next step demonstrates faithfulness toward God. He fell to the ground and worshiped. That's right—he didn't berate God or ask "Why me?" or "Why them?" Instead, he acknowledged that everything comes from God, and he praised the name of the Lord.

Job knew God—really knew him with an uncommon intimacy. His close communion with God had taught him that God was the only one who could give him any kind of real comfort. Job's knowledge yielded a deep trust in an infallible Lord—a trust that enabled Job's heart to keep beating even in the midst of overwhelming heartbreak. It enabled him to respond to terrible pain with worship and praise.

Yes, times of seeking for answers and grappling for understanding followed that day of destruction, but Job's initial response reflected a heart that knew and trusted God. What an amazing and beautiful image!

Jehoshaphat son of Asa became king of Judah in the fourth year of Ahab king of Israel. Jehoshaphat was thirty-five years old when he became king, and he reigned in Jerusalem twenty-five years. His mother's name was Azubah daughter of Shilhi. In everything he walked in the ways of his father Asa and did not stray from them; he did what was right in the eyes of the LORD.

The Bible doesn't describe Jehoshaphat's physical appearance, but it does reveal that he bore a strong family resemblance to his father Asa, who was known for opposing idolatry and worshiping God. Like father, like son. Jehoshaphat was a good and godly king who reigned over Judah for twenty-five years. His epitaph could be summed up in a few poignant words: "Jehoshaphat, who sought the LORD with all his heart" (2 Chronicles 22:9). By following in his godly father's footsteps, King Jehoshaphat pleased God.

Not everyone has had the benefit of a Christian upbringing, but that in no way excludes them from the family of God. God has a way of adopting some of the most unlikely spiritual orphans. He wants you and me and others in the family to adopt them too! We can show them how to live in a holy way just as Asa showed Jehoshaphat.

You may or may not have kids who have inherited your eyes and ears, but you can help others develop eyes to see God and ears to hear the Gospel. Encourage those in your sphere of influence to cultivate a strong family resemblance to their heavenly Father.

Judges 4:4-5

Deborah, a prophetess, the wife of Lappidoth, was leading Israel at that time. She held court under the Palm of Deborah between Ramah and Bethel in the hill country of Ephraim, and the Israelites came to her to have their disputes decided.

Deborah was like a prickly pear cactus. Though she was female, Deborah was given the responsibility of judging the wayward Israelites. To understand her personality, you need to understand her name. Deborah literally means wasp and her story reveals that she was willing to sting if need be, even leading an army to war if the Lord led. This godly woman could be prickly, but she also blessed those who followed the Lord.

Perhaps you know someone who is as prickly as a cactus. The care of prickly pears is quite simple. Put them in the sun and don't overwater them. You can care for your prickly friends the same way. Make sure you place them in the Son by praying for them often. And don't saturate them with too much attention. That's when you might get stung.

Matthew 25:1-13

The kingdom of heaven will be like ten virgins who took their lamps and went out to meet the bridegroom. Five of them were foolish and five were wise. The foolish ones took their lamps but did not take any oil with them. The wise, however, took oil in jars along with their lamps. The bridegroom was a long time in coming, and they all became drowsy and fell asleep.

At midnight the cry rang out. "Here's the bridegroom! Come out to meet him!"

Then all the virgins woke up and trimmed their lamps. The foolish ones said to the wise, "Give us some of your oil; our lamps are going out."

"No," they replied, "there may not be enough for both us and you. Go to those who sell oil and buy some for yourselves."

But while they were on their way to buy the oil, the bridegroom arrived. The virgins who were ready went in with him to the wedding banquet. And the door was shut.

Later the others also came. "Sir! Sir!" they said. "Open the door for us!"

But he replied, "I tell you the truth, I don't know you."

Therefore keep watch, because you do not know the day or the hour.

In the parable of the ten virgins, Jesus encouraged all believers to be like eager bridesmaids, ready and waiting for the coming of the bridegroom. In Jesus' wedding scenario, the wise bridesmaids didn't carry bouquets of flowers; they carried oil-filled lamps.

The ancient Israelites considered marriage to be the greatest of life's events. When the time came for the wedding, the groom and his friends would dress in their finest clothes and parade to the home of the bride, usually by night, to bring the bride and her attendants to the groom's home. This was why it was so important for the bridesmaids to keep oil in their lamps.

But the oil in the lamps holds far more significance than its practical ability to illuminate the path or its romantic quality of providing ambience for the wedding. In Scripture, oil symbolizes the presence of the Holy Spirit. Through this story, Jesus was symbolically reminding people that when he returns, he will be coming for those who are wise enough to be filled with the Holy Spirit. Are you ready? Are you like a wise bridesmaid with oil in your lamp?

After Abram had been living in Canaan ten years, Sarai his wife took her Egyptian maidservant Hagar and gave her to her husband to be his wife. He slept with Hagar, and she conceived.

When she knew she was pregnant, she began to despise her mistress. Then Sarai said to Abram, "You are responsible for the wrong I am suffering. I put my servant in your arms, and now that she knows she is pregnant, she despises me. May the LORD judge between you and me."

"Your servant is in your hands," Abram said. "Do with her whatever you think best." Then Sarai mistreated Hagar; so she fled from her.

The angel of the LORD found Hagar near a spring in the desert; it was the spring that is beside the road to Shur. And he said, "Hagar, servant of Sarai, where have you come from, and where are you going?" "I'm running away from my mistress Sarai," she answered. Then the angel of the LORD told her, "Go back to your mistress and submit to her."

Life at the crossroads

Where have you come from and where are you going? The question came to Hagar at the pinnacle of a crucial decision. She was torn between allegiance to her mistress, Sarai (known as Sarah later in the story), and the innate desire to be free to raise the baby now growing inside of her. As with most questions one faces when standing at one of life's many crossroads, it haunted her. Where had she come from? Where was she going? She concluded that she'd come from a place no woman should have to be. I've come from the grasp of a woman who hates me. I've come from the burden of carrying a baby whose father loves someone else. I've come from a terrifying place of confusion, isolation and abandonment.

She was wandering in the desert, considering her options. Could she make it? Would she die? As if the Lord's angel had traced her thoughts, he cut through her myriad of optional scenarios with a command. "Go back to your mistress and submit to her." The crossroads pointed to a path she did not want to take and had not planned to take. But God had spoken, and Hagar had to obey.

Deuteronomy 22:22

If a man is found sleeping with another man's wife, both the man who slept with her and the woman must die. You must purge the evil from Israel.

God's severe punishment for betrayal can be seen throughout the book of Deuteronomy. And what human betrayal surpasses that of a wife against her husband or vice versa? God instituted a sexual union between man and woman from the beginning of time. Sex was integral to God's plan. Marriage would be a blessing, honorable in every way.

However, what God intended for honor, we often pervert into dishonorable, selfish acts. The enormous capacity for sex to bind two people together also carries an equal capacity to destroy lives when practiced outside God's purpose. The harsh penalties for sexual misconduct confirm the grave importance God placed on sexual intimacy. What many term as "sexual freedom" comes at a very high price.

So if past sexual sin still harrows your soul, accept the love and forgiveness Jesus offers. If you feel guilty for a marital collapse, know that Jesus knows all about it and offers a clean slate. God created you as a beautifully sexual human being. Celebrate that fact, but honor him with it.

They traveled from Mount Hor along the route to the Red Sea, to go around Edom. But the people grew impatient on the way; they spoke against God and against Moses, and said, "Why have you brought us up out of Egypt to die in the desert? There is no bread! There is no water! And we detest this miserable food!"

Then the LORD sent venomous snakes among them; they bit the people and many Israelites died. The people came to Moses and said, "We sinned when we spoke against the LORD and against you. Pray that the LORD will take the snakes away from us." So Moses prayed for the people.

The LORD said to Moses, "Make a snake and put it up on a pole; anyone who is bitten can look at it and live." So Moses made a bronze snake and put it up on a pole. Then when anyone was bitten by a snake and looked at the bronze snake, he lived.

Look up and live

We wonder whether God is really guiding us, whether he really has chosen us. And if he has, why is life so hard? And then we begin to doubt ... just like the Israelites. They tramped through a scorching desert, their feet dusty and sore. They faced yet another day of water rations and a menu of manna. The miracles to get them out of Egypt had been amazing. Yet the way was so rough. It was easy to forget all that. Looking out at the hot desert, it was easy to assume God had left them alone there.

Eventually, the Israelites' grumbling exploded into venomous blasphemy against God. In retribution, God sent a plague of poisonous snakes to stop their poisonous treason. Sometimes God's rebuke might feel like one more reason to resent him. But God's compassion drives his punishments. When his people called out for help—wailing for the cure—he provided a remedy.

Do frustration and discouragement sometimes drive you to mumble and complain? Stop. Look up to Jesus Christ. He took on your sin to heal your heart. He is the only way you can rid yourself of the venom of bitterness. Look up to him and live.

Notes

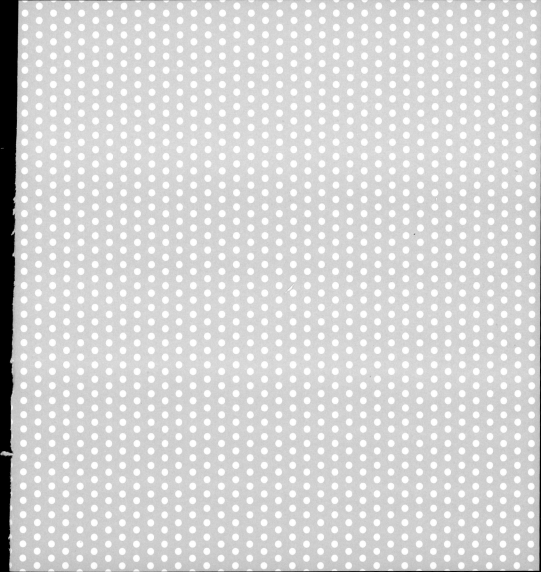

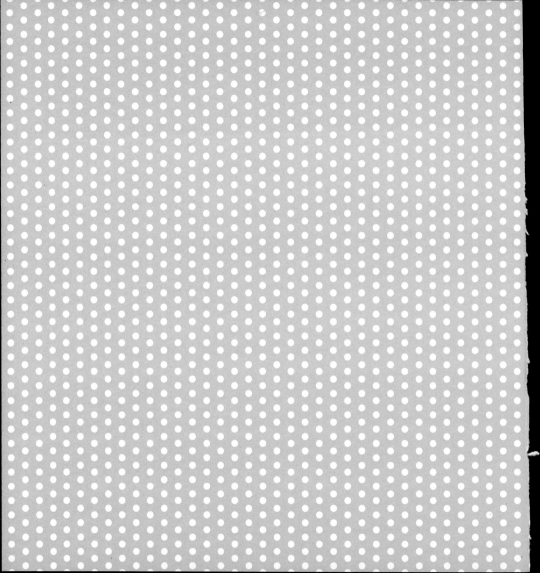